Homestyle VEGAN

EASY, EVERYDAY PLANT-BASED RECIPES

AMBER ST. PETER
FOUNDER OF FETTLE VEGAN

PAGE STREET
PUBLISHING CO.

This book is dedicated to my partner, *Alex,* for always being an honest and willing taste tester and to my pup, *Maddie,* for always cleaning up dropped crumbs from the floor.

I feel pretty lucky to have two creatures who love food just as much as I do in my life.

PAGE STREET
PUBLISHING CO.

Copyright © 2016 Amber St. Peter

First published in 2016 by
Page Street Publishing Co.
27 Congress Street, Suite 105
Salem, MA 01970
www.pagestreetpublishing.com

Distributed by Macmillan, sales in Canada by The Canadian Manda Group.

19 18 17 16   1 2 3 4 5

ISBN-13: 9781624142833
ISBN-10: 1624142834

Library of Congress Control Number: 2016934574

Cover and book design by Page Street Publishing Co.
Photography by Amber St. Peter

Printed and bound in China

Page Street is proud to be a member of 1% for the Planet. Members donate one percent of their sales to one or more of the over 1,500 environmental and sustainability charities across the globe who participate in this program.

Contents

WHEN COOKIES WON'T CUT IT - 131

HAVE A DRINK - 149

STOCK YOUR PANTRY - 165

INTRO

Hi! I'm Amber, the face behind all of these healthier homestyle recipes. I've been plant-based and following a vegan diet for nearly 6 years, but for me it's really all about eating well and saving the planet at the same time. As someone who considers herself an environmentalist, I think eating vegan is an easy way to save the lives of animals while saving ourselves from increasing emissions of greenhouse gases, wasted water and toxic chemicals in our food.

I hope each of these recipes inspires you to try something new. If you are a vegan, you're going to love how easy and satisfying these recipes are. If you're not, they're the perfect way to take your regular meals and health-ify them by removing the meat and dairy, and reducing the amount of sugar in the recipes.

Each of these recipes is here because I really wanted to take traditional, standard American diet foods and make them edible again—and make them easier than ever to whip up. Dishes like my Quinoa Meatball Sub (page 52), French Onion Soup (page 105) and Pumpkin Whoopie Pies (page 129) will change the way you feel about vegan food. They've got tons of texture and flavor, and are sure to impress—plus, you can actually feel good about eating them!

I tried to keep the ingredients in this book simple and attainable as well, because I realize that not everyone has access (or the expendable cash) to go out and buy goji berries and grain-free flours, just to experiment with a recipe you may not love. Every ingredient in this book should be available at your local grocery store, and every recipe will remind you of cooking at home with Mom (or Dad, or Grandma) growing up. Oh, and I promise—NO TOFU! I've revamped the classics, and I can't wait for you to try them!

chapter one

RISE + SHINE

BEEP BEEP BEEP! Yup, that's how most of our mornings start. Slaves to the alarm clock, we roll out of bed, shuffle into the shower, dig through piles of unfolded laundry to find something "work-appropriate" (apparently yoga pants don't qualify?) and grab something less-than-stellar for breakfast as we take off out the door. So let's knock it off, huh? You might not be able to totally ditch the alarm clock but you can set it a little earlier, plan your outfit ahead of time and make one of these easy, start-your-day-right breakfasts. Trust me, it'll make all the difference. Who doesn't wanna get out of bed when the smell of a sweet, healthy, balanced breakfast comes wafting through the room? My Apple Cider Donuts (page 10), Pumpkin Pancakes (page 14) and Peach Cobbler Baked Oatmeal (page 25) will have you doing just that. Let's eat!

APPLE CIDER DONUTS

Growing up in Maine, I would often visit apple orchards in the fall with my elementary school classes to pick apples, press cider and munch as many apple cider donuts as I could get my tiny hands on. Luckily I'm an adult now, so I can pick apples more than once a year and make these delicious homemade donuts anytime I want. This recipe was almost *too* easy to make vegan—simply by using applesauce as a healthier, egg-free binder. You'll have fresh, sweet donuts in half an hour or less!

MAKES 6

1 cup (125 g) all-purpose flour

1 tsp baking powder

1 tsp baking soda

2 tsp (10 g) cinnamon, divided

¼ tsp nutmeg

¼ tsp ground ginger

⅛ tsp salt

½ cup (136 g) Homemade Applesauce (page 181), or store-bought

½ cup (100 g) granulated sugar

¼ cup (60 ml) apple cider

2 tbsp (30 ml) apple cider vinegar

2 tbsp (30 ml) coconut oil, melted, plus more to grease pan

¾ cup (98 g) powdered sugar

Preheat the oven to 375°F (191°C).

In a large mixing bowl, combine the flour, baking powder, baking soda, 1 teaspoon of the cinnamon, nutmeg, ginger and salt.

In a separate mixing bowl, whisk together the applesauce, granulated sugar, apple cider and apple cider vinegar. Mix the dry ingredients into the wet ingredients about a cup at a time, stirring to combine. Pour in the melted coconut oil and whisk to incorporate. Let the mixture set while you grease a 6-mold donut pan with coconut oil.

Once the pan is greased and the oven is preheated, pour the mixture equally among the 6 donut molds and bake for 15 minutes. While the donuts bake, whisk together the powdered sugar and the remaining 1 teaspoon cinnamon in a wide dish.

When the donuts finish cooking, move them to a cooling rack to cool slightly, then roll them in the powdered sugar mixture until they're completely coated. Enjoy immediately!

Leftover donuts keep for 1 to 2 days in an airtight container on the counter, but are best enjoyed fresh.

CORNED BEAN HASH

Corned beef hash was a big holiday food in our family when I was growing up. Obviously, I don't eat beef now, but sometimes I still crave the salty, rich flavor of the hash and how great an addition to breakfast it was. This recipe cleverly uses lighter, healthier kidney beans to mimic the missing protein and tahini for flavor. It's so good, you'll fool even the heartiest of meat-eaters!

SERVES 4

1 cup (230 g) cooked kidney beans

1 tbsp (15 ml) coconut or olive oil

1 clove garlic, minced

1 cup (151 g) finely diced white onion

1 cup (175 g) chopped red potatoes (½" [13 mm]) chunks)

¼ cup (62 g) tahini

1 tbsp (15 ml) soy sauce or coconut aminos

¼ tsp salt

¼ tsp pepper

⅛ tsp cayenne

Chives, for garnish

In a small bowl, mash about three-fourths of the kidney beans with a fork and set aside.

Heat the oil in a large skillet over medium heat. Sauté the garlic and onions for 3 to 5 minutes, or until softened and fragrant. Toss in the potatoes, tahini, soy sauce, salt, pepper and cayenne, stirring to combine.

Cover and continue to cook over medium heat for 15 to 20 minutes, or until the potatoes are fork-tender. If things start getting stuck to the pan before the potatoes are ready, you can add 1 tablespoon (15 ml) of water as needed to loosen things up. Once the mixture is becoming browned and crispy, remove from the heat. Garnish with fresh chives and serve!

Leftovers can be refrigerated and reheated as needed for up to 1 week.

PUMPKIN PANCAKES

There is almost no better way to start your day than with sweet, golden pancakes. Trust me on this one. The only way to make perfect pancakes even better? Throw a little pumpkin in! They're fluffy, light and packed full of pumpkin spice—you'd never know they're vegan. These pancakes will be your new fall obsession!

MAKES 8

¾ cup (94 g) all-purpose flour

⅓ cup (43 g) whole wheat flour

½ tsp baking powder

½ tsp pumpkin pie spice

¼ tsp cinnamon

¼ tsp nutmeg

¼ tsp ground ginger

⅛ tsp salt

1½ cups (360 ml) unsweetened almond milk

⅓ cup (75 g) pumpkin puree

1 tbsp (15 ml) maple syrup

Vegan butter or oil, to grease pan

In a large mixing bowl, whisk together the flours, baking powder, pumpkin pie spice, cinnamon, nutmeg, ginger and salt. Make a well in the center of the dry ingredients and pour in the milk, pumpkin puree and maple syrup. Whisk until completely combined, then set aside.

Heat a large, lightly greased skillet over medium heat. Pour ¼ cup (60 ml) scoops of batter onto the skillet and cook for about 2 minutes per side, until golden. Adjust the temperature as necessary while cooking because the pan will continue to heat up over time.

Serve the pancakes with vegan butter and maple syrup!

OLD-FASHIONED CINNAMON ROLLS WITH WALNUTS + VANILLA BEAN GLAZE

There is nothing better for breakfast or brunch than a huge, ooey-gooey cinnamon roll dripping with icing and speckled with walnuts. This is the kind of breakfast that actually makes you WANT to get out of bed on a Saturday morning. It's the epitome of comfort food, and when paired with homemade vanilla bean glaze? *Girrrrrrrl!* Go preheat your oven.

MAKES 9

CINNAMON ROLLS

1 cup (240 ml) unsweetened almond milk, at room temperature

¼ cup (60 g) vegan butter, melted

2¼ tsp (7 g) active dry yeast

3 cups (375 g) all-purpose flour

1 tbsp (12 g) granulated sugar

¼ tsp salt

Olive oil or coconut oil, for greasing

TOPPING

¼ cup (60 g) vegan butter, melted

¼ cup (50 g) granulated sugar

2 tsp (5 g) cinnamon

¼ cup (29 g) chopped walnuts

VANILLA BEAN GLAZE

1 cup (130 g) powdered sugar

2 vanilla beans, scraped

2 tbsp (30 ml) unsweetened almond milk

Chopped walnuts, for garnish

To make the cinnamon rolls, combine the almond milk and melted vegan butter in the bowl of a stand mixer. Pour in the yeast and let sit to activate, about 5 to 10 minutes.

Meanwhile, combine the flour, granulated sugar and salt in a medium-size mixing bowl. When the yeast mixture is ready, pour the flour mixture in about 1 cup (125 g) at a time, stirring as you go.

When the dough comes together, knead with a dough hook for about 1 minute, to form a loose, sticky ball. You can add a little bit of almond milk here, if needed, to keep the dough sticky. Move the dough ball to a lightly oiled bowl, cover with plastic wrap or a clean dish towel and leave in a warm place to double in size, 1 to 2 hours.

Turn the dough out onto a lightly floured surface and roll out to a ¼-inch (6-mm) thick rectangle.

For the topping, brush the dough generously with the melted butter, then sprinkle the granulated sugar, cinnamon and walnuts evenly all over the top. Starting on one side, roll the dough into a thick log.

Using a serrated or very sharp knife, slice into 9 equal rolls. Place the rolls into a well-greased 8 x 8-inch (20 x 20-cm) baking dish, cover with plastic wrap or a clean dish towel and let sit by the oven to rise for about 30 more minutes.

Preheat the oven to 350°F (177°C). Bake the rolls for 25 to 30 minutes, until golden and fluffy. While the rolls bake, prepare the glaze by whisking together the powdered sugar, vanilla bean scrapings and milk until smooth. Once completely cooled, drizzle the vanilla bean glaze generously over the top and garnish with chopped walnuts. Enjoy!

BAKED BREAKFAST GRATIN

I've made a few gratins since going vegan, but they always turned out too goopy or mushy—or on the other hand, dried out and undercooked—I just couldn't seem to get it right. This gratin, though? Total SUCCESS! The key is super thinly sliced potatoes and an extra creamy, super rich cheese sauce. The tangy and smoky flavors come together to make a decadent brunch dish or Sunday morning breakfast in bed. You'll go back for seconds!

SERVES 6 TO 8

Olive oil or coconut oil, for greasing

1¼ cups (300 ml) unsweetened almond milk

½ cup (123 g) plain vegan yogurt

½ cup (52 g) nutritional yeast

2 tbsp (15 g) cornstarch

1 tsp salt

¾ tsp smoked paprika

½ tsp pepper

¼ tsp cayenne pepper

2 lb (910 g) red potatoes, sliced ⅛" to ¼" (3 to 6 mm) thick

1 cup (175 g) finely diced red bell pepper

¾ cup (151 g) finely diced red onion

4 cloves garlic, minced

Chives, for garnish

Preheat the oven to 350°F (177°C). Grease a 9 x 13-inch (23 x 33-cm) baking dish.

In a medium-size mixing bowl, whisk together the milk, yogurt, nutritional yeast, cornstarch, salt, smoked paprika, pepper and cayenne pepper. Set aside.

Layer about half of the potatoes into the greased baking dish, spreading them evenly. Sprinkle about half of each of the bell peppers, onions and garlic over the potatoes, then top with about half of the wet mixture. Layer the rest of the potatoes on top of that, followed by the rest of the peppers, onions and garlic. Pour the last half of the wet mixture over the top. Bake for 50 to 60 minutes, until golden and bubbly. Garnish with chives and serve!

APPLE CINNAMON DUTCH BABY WITH CRUMBLED WALNUTS

Pancakes are yummy and donuts are great, but this sweet, crunchy, gooey Dutch baby is LIFE-CHANGING. Intended as a dish for sharing, this recipe is perfect for a group brunch or after a morning of heavy drinking. I cut the sugar way down from the original recipe, but it still packs enough sweetness to cure your sweet tooth and impress your friends.

SERVES 6

4 tbsp (28 g) ground flax

½ cup + 2 tbsp (150 ml) warm water

2 cups (240 g) whole wheat flour

2 cups (475 ml) nondairy milk

1 tsp vanilla extract

½ cup (136 g) Homemade Applesauce (page 181), or store-bought

2 tbsp (14 g) cinnamon, divided

¼ cup (50 g) granulated sugar

¼ cup (40 g) brown sugar

1 tsp nutmeg

½ cup (60 g) walnuts, finely chopped or crumbled

4 tbsp (60 ml) vegan butter or coconut oil

2 medium-size tart apples, cored and thinly sliced

Maple syrup or powdered sugar, for garnish

Preheat the oven to 400°F (205°C).

In a small bowl, whisk together the ground flax and water. Set aside to thicken.

In a large mixing bowl, whisk together the flour, milk, vanilla, applesauce, thickened flax mixture and 1 tablespoon (7 g) of the cinnamon.

In a separate, smaller bowl, mix together the granulated sugar, brown sugar, remaining 1 tablespoon (7 g) cinnamon, nutmeg and walnuts. Set aside.

Place the vegan butter into an 8-inch (20-cm) cast-iron pan and place it in the oven. Heat until the butter completely melts, about 3 minutes, then remove the pan from the oven and pour in the batter. Place the pan back into the oven and bake for 20 to 22 minutes, until the Dutch baby is cooked about halfway through and the sides are beginning to puff up. Pull it from the oven and cover it in apple slices. Spread the sugar and nut mixture over the top, and put the pan back into the oven. Bake 20 to 25 more minutes, then remove the pan from the oven.

Serve slices immediately with a drizzle of maple syrup or a dusting of powdered sugar.

Leftovers can be kept for up to 3 days, covered, in the fridge.

FLUFFY SATURDAY MORNING WAFFLES

Waffles without fluffy, whipped egg whites?! You betcha! You don't need any eggs to make these super fluffy, healthier waffles that taste great, too. The flax here works as both a binder and a healthy addition of omegas . . . which means you can have extra maple syrup on top, right?

MAKES 4

1½ cups (360 ml) unsweetened almond milk

1½ tbsp (22 ml) apple cider vinegar

¼ cup (60 ml) melted coconut oil

2 tbsp (30 ml) maple syrup

1 tsp vanilla extract

2 cups (310 g) whole wheat pastry flour

2 tbsp (6 g) ground flax

1 tbsp (11 g) baking powder

⅛ tsp salt

Maple syrup and vegan butter, for serving

Fresh fruit, for garnish

Preheat your waffle iron and spray a bit of oil or nonstick spray onto it.

Combine the unsweetened almond milk and apple cider vinegar in a measuring cup and leave to curdle, about 5 minutes. Meanwhile, whisk together the melted coconut oil, maple syrup and vanilla. Pour in the curdled milk mixture and whisk to combine.

In a medium-size mixing bowl, whisk together the whole wheat pastry flour, ground flax, baking powder and salt.

Pour the wet mixture into the dry, stirring to completely combine. Let the batter sit for at least 10 minutes to aerate (see Tip).

Pour ½-cup (120-ml) scoops of batter onto the waffle iron (adjust as necessary for the size of your waffle maker) and cook until the waffle is golden and cooked through, 3 to 5 minutes.

Top with vegan butter and maple syrup and serve with fresh fruit!

Leftover waffles can be kept in the fridge but are really best enjoyed fresh.

Tip

Letting the batter sit before putting it into the waffle iron is essential—it gives your batter time to aerate and makes for a much better, fluffier waffle.

PEACH COBBLER BAKED OATMEAL

This dish is super easy to whip up and will absolutely be the best thing at your breakfast table! It serves a big group and would be perfect alongside a large tray of mimosas and a bunch of fresh fruit. It has become a favorite around my place because it's easily made the night before and makes brunching as stress-free and delicious as it should be.

SERVES 8

3 tbsp (20 g) ground flax

½ cup (120 ml) water

3 cups (675 g) pitted and chopped peaches (1" [2.5 cm] chunks)

½ cup (80 g) almonds, roughly chopped

3 cups (325 g) old-fashioned oats

2 tsp (7 g) baking powder

½ tsp salt

1½ cups (360 ml) unsweetened almond milk

1 (14-oz [400-ml]) can full-fat coconut milk

½ cup packed (110 g) brown sugar

1 tsp vanilla extract

1 tsp freshly ground nutmeg

1 tsp cinnamon

Preheat the oven to 350°F (175°C).

Begin by mixing together the ground flax and water in a small bowl; set aside to let the mixture gelatinize and turn to an egglike consistency, about 5 minutes. While you wait, chop up the peaches and almonds. Set these aside, too.

In a large mixing bowl, combine the oats, baking powder and salt. Add the chopped peaches and about half of the chopped almonds.

In a separate bowl, whisk together the flax "egg" mixture, almond milk, coconut milk, brown sugar, vanilla, nutmeg and cinnamon. Pour the wet ingredients into the dry ingredients, stirring to combine and uniformly distribute the peaches and almonds.

Pour the mixture into an 8 x 8-inch or 9 x 9-inch (20 x 20-cm or 23 x 23-cm) baking dish and top with the remaining almonds. Bake for 45 to 55 minutes, until the mixture is bubbling and the edges have slightly crisped. Serve with a drizzle of maple syrup or a little warm milk. Enjoy!

This keeps well in an airtight container in the fridge for up to 1 week. It reheats well in the microwave or covered in foil and reheated in a warm oven.

EASY ORANGE-SCENTED GRANOLA

I try to avoid sugary breakfasts—they set a bad tone for the whole day! This easy, healthy, crunchy granola is the perfect way to avoid falling into a crummy breakfast pattern. Whip up a batch on Sunday and you've got simple, ready-to-eat breakfasts for every morning of the week! And the best part? This recipe uses just a little sugar to sweeten the batch, which you can easily leave out for a totally refined sugar–free morning.

MAKES ABOUT 6 CUPS (730 G)

¼ cup (50 g) sugar

Zest of 1 orange (about 1 tsp, packed)

3 cups (241 g) old-fashioned rolled oats

1 cup (120 g) almonds, sliced or roughly chopped

1 cup (150 g) cashews, roughly chopped

1 cup (120 g) pecans, roughly chopped

1 cup (76 g) flaked coconut

½ cup (94 g) chia seeds

½ tsp cinnamon

½ tsp salt

¼ cup (60 ml) maple syrup

¼ cup (60 ml) coconut oil, melted

Preheat the oven to 350°F (175°C). Line a baking sheet with parchment paper.

In a small bowl, use your fingers to mix together the sugar and orange zest until fragrant. Set aside.

In a large bowl, mix together the rolled oats, almonds, cashews, pecans, flaked coconut, chia seeds, cinnamon and salt. Pour in the orange-scented sugar, the maple syrup and the melted coconut oil, and stir to coat evenly.

Pour the mixture onto the baking sheet, using the back of a wooden spoon to press the granola down firmly so chunks will form. Bake for 20 to 30 minutes, stirring halfway through. To encourage a chunkier granola, press the granola down again with a spoon after stirring. When finished, let the granola cool completely before moving it to an airtight container. Serve with nondairy milk and fresh fruit!

chapter two

MEALS THAT'LL STICK TO YOUR RIBS

Sometimes a bowl of soup or a simple salad just won't cut it. If you've been working hard and have a rumbling tummy, then you've come to the right place. These dishes all have plenty of protein and flavor, and serve at least four. These are meals that'll warm you up, fill your tummy and keep you satisfied all day long. Dishes like my Chick'un + Dumplings (page 30), Red Beans + Rice Gumbo (page 38) and Tomato Basil Soup with Cornbread Croutons (page 34) make great leftovers for next-day lunches and are something the whole family can sit down and enjoy. You won't leave the table feeling hungry after one of these meals, so loosen your belt and let's eat!

CHICK'UN + DUMPLINGS

Chicken and veggies smothered in gravy and topped with buttery dumplings was my FAVORITE childhood meal. I could've eaten it every night for dinner, if Mom would've let me. Lucky for me, I have this amazing, way healthier version to eat now. And no one can tell me NOT to eat it every night for dinner! You'll be amazed at how much flavor comes from a dish with such little work. The chickpeas are a perfect replacement for chicken, and my buttery vegan biscuits are the perfect stand-in for dumplings. You are going to LOVE this meal!

SERVES 6

1 batch Fluffy Whole Wheat Biscuits (page 166), cut out but uncooked

1 tbsp (15 ml) olive oil

2 cloves garlic, minced

1 cup (170 g) chopped yellow onion

3 cups (475 g) frozen mixed green beans, carrots, corn and peas (or sub fresh!)

1¼ cups (225 g) cooked chickpeas

½ cup (62 g) all-purpose flour

2¼ cups (540 ml) vegetable broth

½ cup (120 ml) unsweetened almond milk

2 bay leaves

1 tsp salt

½ tsp pepper

Preheat the oven to 425°F (218°C). Set the uncooked biscuits in the fridge until ready to use.

Heat the olive oil in a large saucepan over medium heat. Add the garlic and onion and sauté until soft, 5 to 7 minutes. Add the mixed vegetables, chickpeas and flour and stir well. Pour in the vegetable broth and unsweetened almond milk and whisk to combine. Finally, add the bay leaves, salt and pepper and simmer the mixture until thickened, about 10 minutes.

Once the sauce has thickened, remove the bay leaves and discard. Pour the mixture into a 9 x 13-inch (23 x 33-cm) baking dish. Place the uncooked biscuits on top, spacing them as evenly as possible.

Bake for 20 to 25 minutes, until the mixture is bubbling and the biscuits are golden. Let cool for 5 minutes before serving.

Leftovers will keep in the fridge for up to 1 week.

Tip

You can make the filling and biscuits ahead of time and just keep them separately in the fridge until you're ready to cook.

BACON-LESS BAKED BEANS

I've always loved baked beans but had only ever really had them from a can. After making this recipe, I'll never go back! These beans are savory, full of flavor and impressively easy to make. You'll never miss the meat! This recipe is going to become your new go-to comfort food meal.

SERVES 6 TO 8

1 tbsp (15 ml) coconut or olive oil

2 cloves garlic, minced

1 large onion, chopped

1 medium red bell pepper, cored and chopped

¾ cup (170 ml) ketchup

¾ cup (170 ml) tomato sauce (I use Garlic Herb Pizza + Pasta Sauce [page 173])

½ cup (110 g) firmly packed brown sugar

¼ cup (60 ml) apple cider vinegar

1 tbsp (15 ml) liquid smoke

1 tbsp (15 ml) soy sauce or coconut aminos

½ tsp salt

¼ tsp pepper

¼ tsp cayenne pepper

6 cups (1020 g) or about 4 (14-oz [392-g]) cans cooked pinto beans

Preheat the oven to 325°F (163°C).

Heat the oil over medium heat in a large oven-safe pot or Dutch oven. Sauté the garlic, onion and bell pepper together until softened, about 5 minutes.

Add the ketchup, tomato sauce, brown sugar, vinegar, liquid smoke, soy sauce, salt, pepper and cayenne and simmer for about 5 minutes, stirring occasionally. Pour in the pinto beans and stir to combine.

Place a cover on the pot and put the pot into the oven. Bake for 1 hour, then remove the lid and bake for 30 more minutes to thicken. Remove from the oven and serve immediately!

Leftover beans will keep in an airtight container in the fridge for up to 1 week.

TOMATO BASIL SOUP WITH CORNBREAD CROUTONS

Unlike Campbell's cans, this soup is loaded with fresh vegetables, flavorful herbs and a secret ingredient—homemade cashew cream! It adds a richness in texture and slight nutty flavor that brings this soup from average to excellent. It's simple to prepare and even easier to reheat later. Tastes best alongside a gooey grilled cheese sandwich!

SERVES 8

SOUP

1 cup (150 g) cashews

1 cup (240 ml) water, plus more for soaking

4 tbsp (60 g) vegan butter

6 cloves garlic, minced

2 medium yellow onions, chopped

2½ lb (1.1 kg) tomatoes, chopped

4 cups (950 ml) vegetable broth

2 bay leaves

½ cup packed (40 g) fresh basil

1 tsp salt

½ tsp pepper

CROUTONS

3 heaping cups (330 g) stale cornbread (½" [1.3 cm] cubes)

1 tsp olive oil

¼ tsp salt

¼ tsp pepper

To make the soup, soak the cashews in enough warm water to cover for at least 30 minutes. Drain the water off, pour the cashews into a blender and pour in the 1 cup (240 ml) water. Blend until creamy. Set aside.

Preheat the oven to 400°F (205°C). Line a baking sheet with parchment paper.

In a large soup pot or Dutch oven, melt the butter over medium heat. Add the garlic and onions and sauté for about 5 minutes, until softened and fragrant. Add the tomatoes and cook for 10 more minutes, stirring occasionally. Pour in the vegetable broth, bay leaves, basil, salt and pepper and simmer for 30 to 60 minutes.

While the soup cooks, prepare the cornbread croutons by spreading the cubed bread over the prepared baking sheet. Drizzle with olive oil, sprinkle with salt and pepper and bake for about 15 minutes, flipping halfway through, until crisp.

When the soup is ready, discard the bay leaves and pour the cashew cream into the pot. Using an immersion or high-speed blender, blend the soup in batches until creamy.

Serve hearty bowls of soup sprinkled with the cornbread croutons and cracked black pepper!

Leftovers will keep in the fridge for up to 1 week.

VEGETABLE POT PIE

Pot pies stuffed with seasonal vegetables are the best. Easy to make and even easier to eat up, they come together quickly and have plenty of room for experimentation. This healthier, meat-free version topped with a buttery crust has become a go-to weeknight dinner in our house!

SERVES 6

CRUST

2¼ cups (281 g) all-purpose flour

1 tbsp (15 g) sugar

1 tsp salt

½ cup (115 g) cold vegan butter or coconut oil

⅓ to ½ cup (80 to 120 ml) ice water

FILLING

1 tbsp (15 ml) olive oil

2 cloves garlic, minced

1 cup (150 g) chopped yellow onion

3 cups (475 g) frozen mixed green beans, carrots, corn and peas (or sub fresh!)

1 cup (225 g) cubed red potatoes (½" [1.3 cm] cubes)

½ cup (63 g) all-purpose flour

2 cups (480 ml) vegetable broth

2 bay leaves

1 tsp salt

½ tsp pepper

1 tbsp (15 g) vegan butter, melted

Preheat the oven to 400°F (205°C). Grease an 8 x 8-inch (20 x 20-cm) square baking dish.

Prepare the crust by combining the flour, sugar and salt in a large mixing bowl. Cut in the cold butter with a pastry cutter or fork until small crumbs form. Drizzle in the ice water, using a wooden spoon to stir the mixture together until a dough forms. Wrap the dough in plastic wrap and stick it in the fridge to chill.

To prepare the filling, heat the olive oil in a large saucepan over medium heat. Add the garlic and onion and sauté until soft, 5 to 7 minutes. Add the mixed vegetables and potatoes and stir to combine. Next, add in the flour and stir to coat the vegetables. Then, whisk in the vegetable broth. Finally, add the bay leaves, salt and pepper and simmer the mixture until thickened, about 10 minutes.

While the mixture thickens, remove the crust from the fridge and turn it out onto a lightly floured surface. Split the dough into two halves. Roll them out to about ¼-inch (6-mm) thickness, and press one half of the dough into the greased baking dish, being sure to cover the dish completely. Set the other rolled-out dough aside for the top layer of the pie.

Once the sauce has thickened, remove the bay leaves and discard. Pour the thickened vegetable filling into the crust-lined baking dish. Carefully place the second crust over the top, using a fork or your fingers to press together the edges. Poke a few small holes in the top for steam to escape using a fork or a toothpick. Brush the top generously with the melted vegan butter.

Bake the pie for 30 to 40 minutes, or until the crust is golden. Let cool for 5 minutes before cutting and serving.

Leftovers will keep in the fridge for up to 1 week, and can be frozen indefinitely.

Tip

You can make the filling and crust ahead of time and just keep them separately in the fridge until you're ready to cook.

RED BEANS + RICE GUMBO

This is a real "stick-to-your-ribs" kind of meal. It's hearty, a little spicy and super delicious. My version is a meat-free spin on a traditional gumbo, served over fluffy brown rice. It's much healthier for you and is the perfect recipe to pass on to all those friends wondering, "Are you eating enough protein?"

SERVES 8

RICE

1 cup (211 g) uncooked brown rice

2 cups (480 ml) water

Pinch of salt

GUMBO

3 tbsp (45 g) vegan butter or coconut oil

3 tbsp (23 g) all-purpose flour

1 large onion, chopped

2 medium red bell peppers, cored and chopped

2 medium sweet potatoes, cut into 1" (2.5 cm) cubes

2 medium carrots, thinly sliced

2 small chile peppers, diced small

3 cloves garlic, minced

1 tsp smoked paprika

1 tsp Cajun seasoning

¼ tsp salt

¼ tsp pepper

3 cups (700 ml) vegetable broth

6 cups (1020 g) or about 4 (14-oz [392-g]) cans cooked red kidney beans

Fresh parsley and avocado, for garnish

To make the rice, combine the uncooked brown rice, water and salt in a medium-size pot and bring to a boil. Cover, reduce the heat and simmer for 50 to 60 minutes, until all the water has been absorbed. Fluff with a fork and set aside.

While the rice cooks, make the gumbo. Melt the butter in a large Dutch oven over medium heat. Create a roux by whisking in the flour and stirring occasionally for 5 to 7 minutes, until the mixture turns a dark caramel color.

Add the onion, bell peppers, sweet potatoes, carrots, chile peppers and garlic. Cover and sauté for 8 to 10 minutes.

Add the smoked paprika, Cajun seasoning, salt, pepper, vegetable broth and beans and simmer for about 30 minutes, until the veggies are fork-tender and the mixture has thickened. Serve over rice with fresh parsley and avocado slices!

HEARTY 3-BEAN CHILI

Chili was one of the first meals I learned to make for myself after moving out on my own. It's cheap and easy and tastes great with just about any combination of veggies and beans. This version has become a staple in our house, especially in the winter. It whips up quickly, makes great leftovers and somehow tastes *even better* after sitting in the fridge for a day or two. This'll be your new favorite chili!

SERVES 8

1 tbsp (15 ml) coconut or olive oil

4 cloves garlic, minced

2 medium yellow onions, chopped

3 medium bell peppers, cored and diced

1 or 2 jalapeño peppers, seeded and finely diced

1½ lb (700 g) tomatoes, diced

2 heaping cups (285 g) cooked kidney beans

2 heaping cups (285 g) cooked pinto beans

2 heaping cups (285 g) cooked black beans

1 cup (240 ml) vegetable broth or water

1 cup (175 g) fresh or frozen corn kernels

1 tbsp (6 g) cumin

2 tsp (10 g) salt

1 tsp smoked paprika

½ tsp chili powder

Fresh cilantro and avocado, for garnish

Heat the oil in a large soup pot or Dutch oven over medium heat. Sauté the garlic, onions, bell peppers and jalapeños until softened, about 5 minutes.

Pour in the tomatoes, beans, vegetable broth, corn and spices and stir to combine. Simmer over medium heat for 30 to 40 minutes, until the chili thickens and comes together. Serve with fresh cilantro and avocado slices!

Leftovers can be refrigerated and reheated as needed for up to 1 week.

BULGUR WHEAT SALAD WITH ROASTED PARSNIPS, DELICATA SQUASH, SHALLOTS + GRAVY

This recipe is all about trying new vegetables. Parsnips, carrot's pale cousin, are full of flavor and taste great alongside sweet roasted delicata squash and smothered in rich, salty gravy. It's a dish you never knew you would love and is a great comfort food alternative for sneaking more vegetables into your diet!

SERVES 4

BULGUR WHEAT SALAD

1 cup (180 g) uncooked red bulgur

2 cups (480 ml) water

1 medium delicata squash, halved with seeds scooped out

2 medium parsnips, ends trimmed

6 small shallots

2 tbsp (30 ml) olive oil

¾ tsp salt

½ tsp pepper

GRAVY

2 tbsp (29 g) vegan butter

¼ cup (40 g) whole wheat flour

2 cups (480 ml) vegetable broth

¾ tsp truffle salt (sea salt works, too!)

½ tsp chopped fresh thyme

¼ tsp garlic powder

¼ tsp onion powder

Fresh thyme sprigs, for garnish

Preheat the oven to 400°F (205°C).

To make the bulgur wheat salad, combine the bulgur and water in a pot and bring to a boil. Cover, reduce the heat and simmer until tender, about 10 minutes. Drain off excess liquid and fluff the bulgur with a fork. Set aside to cool.

Slice the delicata squash into ½-inch (13-mm) slices and lay on a parchment-lined baking sheet. Thinly slice the parsnips and trim the shallots, leaving them whole, and place them on the baking sheet with the squash. Drizzle the vegetables with the olive oil, using your fingers or tongs to evenly coat them. Sprinkle the salt and pepper evenly over the vegetables. Roast for 20 to 25 minutes, flipping about halfway through.

While the vegetables cook, make the gravy. Melt the butter in a small saucepan. Whisk in the flour and cook over medium heat until the mixture browns, about 5 minutes, creating a roux. Pour in the vegetable broth, salt, thyme, garlic powder and onion powder and whisk to combine. Bring the mixture to a boil, then reduce the heat and simmer for 10 to 15 minutes, stirring occasionally, until the gravy thickens.

When the vegetables are ready, serve them over the cooked bulgur and drizzle with gravy. Garnish with a sprig of fresh thyme!

Tip
You can sub in other veggies here for the parsnips and delicata squash, if you like!

APPLE FENNEL STUFFING WITH CARAMELIZED ONIONS

For years, the only stuffing I'd ever eaten was the weird, kinda mushy from-a-box version that only came out at our place on Thanksgiving and Easter. And it was okay, but I had no idea what I was missing. I don't remember the first time I had a crusty, moist homemade stuffing, but it changed my mind forever. Once you've had the real thing, you just can't go back—and with this easy recipe, you'll never have to!

SERVES 8

8 cups (350 g) cubed stale sourdough bread (½" [1.3 cm] cubes)

1 medium yellow onion, thinly sliced

1 tsp plus 1 tbsp (15 ml) olive oil, divided

4 cloves garlic, minced

2 celery stalks, thinly sliced

1 medium bulb fennel, cored and chopped

2 medium red apples, cored and chopped

8 sprigs thyme, stems removed

6 fresh sage leaves, finely chopped, plus more for garnish

1 tsp salt

1 tsp pepper

2 cups (480 ml) vegetable broth

Preheat the oven to 350°F (175°C). Place the stale, cubed bread in a large mixing bowl and set aside.

In a small cast-iron or frying pan, combine the onion and 1 teaspoon of the olive oil over low heat. Sauté until caramelized and browned, stirring occasionally and adding water as needed if the onions begin to stick, 20 to 25 minutes.

While the onions caramelize, heat the remaining 1 tablespoon (15 ml) olive oil in a large cast-iron or frying pan over medium heat. Add in the garlic, celery and fennel and cook for 3 to 4 minutes, until slightly softened. Add the apples, thyme, sage, salt and pepper and cook for about 5 more minutes, stirring occasionally. Turn off the heat and pour in the caramelized onions.

Pour the contents of the pan into the bowl with the cubed bread and stir to combine. Add the vegetable broth and mix until the bread is evenly moist.

Pour the entire mixture into a 9 x 13-inch (23 x 33-cm) baking dish or medium-size Dutch oven and bake for 30 minutes, until the stuffing becomes golden brown on top and fragrant. Serve immediately, garnished with sage leaves.

To reheat, you can place the entire baking dish back into the oven covered in foil, removing the foil about halfway through cooking. Or if you have a microwave, feel free to use that. Leftovers will keep for 1 week in the fridge.

GREEN BEAN CASSEROLE WITH CRUNCHY ONIONS

This is a great dish to bring to your family over the holidays. It's scrumptious! The rich mushroom gravy and crunchy onions will remind them of the traditional version, but you can happily remind them that your version is way healthier, and you are an awesome cook. Look at you, conquering the holidays like it ain't no thang!

SERVES 6 TO 8

GREEN BEAN CASSEROLE

1 lb (470 g) green beans, ends trimmed

1 medium head cauliflower, broken into florets

1½ cups (360 ml) unsweetened almond milk

3 tbsp (20 g) nutritional yeast

1 tbsp (9 g) cornstarch

1 tsp chopped fresh thyme, plus sprigs for garnish

1 tsp salt

1 tsp pepper, divided

2 cloves garlic

1 tbsp (15 g) vegan butter

8 oz (227 g) cremini mushrooms, halved and sliced

2 tsp (10 ml) soy sauce or coconut aminos

CRUNCHY ONIONS

1 cup (125 g) all-purpose flour

1 cup (240 ml) unsweetened almond milk

1 cup (110 g) panko bread crumbs

1 tsp salt

¾ tsp garlic powder

1 large onion, thinly sliced

To make the casserole, place the green beans in a steamer basket over a pot of boiling water and cover. Steam for 5 to 6 minutes, until tender. Set aside.

In the same basket, steam the cauliflower florets until tender, 7 to 8 minutes. Pour the steamed florets into a high-speed blender or food processor along with the milk, nutritional yeast, cornstarch, thyme, salt, ½ teaspoon of the pepper and garlic. Blend until smooth. Set aside.

In a large frying pan, melt the butter over medium heat. Sauté the mushrooms, soy sauce and remaining ½ teaspoon pepper together until tender, 3 to 4 minutes. Stir in the cauliflower sauce and green beans and heat together for about 5 minutes, stirring occasionally. Remove from the heat and pour the mixture into a large casserole baking dish—8 x 8-inches (20 x 20-cm) or larger. Set aside.

Preheat the oven to 400°F (205°C). Line a baking sheet with parchment paper.

To make the crunchy onions, pour the flour into a small bowl and the milk into a separate small bowl. In a third bowl, mix together the panko bread crumbs, salt and garlic powder. One or two at a time, dip the onion rings into the flour, coating them completely. Dip them in the milk and then into the panko mixture, tossing to coat. Place them onto the prepared baking sheet. Repeat until all the onions have been dipped.

Place the baking sheet and the casserole into the oven, on different racks. Bake for 25 minutes, then put the crunchy baked onions onto the casserole and bake for another 5 to 10 minutes, until the casserole is bubbling and the onions are crispy. Serve with a sprig of fresh thyme!

CREAMY WILD MUSHROOM SOUP

I used to vehemently despise mushrooms. The real problem was just that I had never had them prepared in a way I liked. This soup was a revelation! The earthy, umami mushroom flavor works so well when tempered with the mild cashew cream and fresh thyme. It's so rich and creamy, no one will miss the dairy. You might even convince a few fungi-haters to change their minds!

SERVES 6 TO 8

¾ cup (130 g) raw cashews

¾ cup (180 ml) warm water

2 tbsp (30 ml) olive oil

2 cloves garlic, minced

1 large yellow onion, chopped

½ lb (227 g) assorted mushrooms, roughly chopped (see Tip)

¼ cup (60 ml) good-quality cooking sherry

3 cups (720 ml) vegetable broth

1½ tsp (3 g) chopped fresh thyme, plus more for garnish

1 tbsp (15 g) plus ⅛ teaspoon salt, divided

1 tsp ground pepper

In a medium-size bowl, soak the cashews in the warm water. Set them aside to soften.

In a large soup pot or Dutch oven, heat the olive oil over medium heat. Sauté the garlic, onion and mushrooms until softened and fragrant, about 5 minutes. Pour in the sherry and continue cooking for about 5 more minutes, stirring occasionally, until the sherry liquid reduces by about half. Pour in the vegetable broth, fresh thyme, 1 tablespoon (15 g) of the salt and pepper and simmer for 20 to 30 minutes.

While the soup simmers, make the cashew cream by blending the soaked cashews, the water they're soaking in and the remaining ⅛ teaspoon salt to create a thick cream. Pour into the simmering soup, and remove the soup from the heat. Using an immersion or high-speed blender, carefully blend the soup in batches. Garnish with fresh thyme. Serve immediately or keep refrigerated and reheat as needed for up to 1 week.

Tip

You can use whatever type of mushrooms you prefer. I've used wild foraged mushrooms, cremini, button, or a mix! It's all delicious.

chapter three

FEED YOUR FRIENDS

Sometimes you just gotta step your game up. Whenever we have friends coming over for a special holiday gathering, to watch Sunday's big game or even just for an afternoon hang, I like it to look like I tried a lot harder than I did. This is actually pretty easily done by shoving your visible mess into an underused closet and whipping up some impressive-looking snackable foods for your guests. Recipes like Quinoa Meatball Sub with Grilled Onions + Peppers (page 52), Buffalo Cauliflower Bites (page 57) and Heirloom Tomato + Hemp Gazpacho (page 58) take plant-based comfort food to the next level and will definitely impress your pals.

QUINOA MEATBALL SUB WITH GRILLED ONIONS + PEPPERS

This delicious take on a traditional meatball sub is healthier, tastier and packed with protein. I use quinoa and chickpeas to give this dish just as much protein as a typical sub would have, except this hearty sandwich comes guilt-free and nearly fat-free, too! It is smothered in tangy homemade tomato sauce and perfectly grilled onions and peppers, and you won't miss anything about the original after a bite of this savory sub.

MAKES 24 MEATBALLS, SERVES 4 TO 6

QUINOA MEATBALLS

1 tbsp (7 g) ground flax

3 tbsp (45 ml) warm water

1 tsp olive oil

4 cloves garlic, minced

2½ cups (402 g) cooked quinoa

½ cup (17 g) loosely packed fresh basil, chopped

¼ cup (8 g) loosely packed fresh oregano, chopped

½ cup (48 g) panko bread crumbs

1 cup (200 g) cooked chickpeas

½ tsp salt

¼ tsp red pepper flakes

GRILLED ONIONS + PEPPERS

1 tsp olive oil

1 large onion, thinly sliced

1 medium red bell pepper, cored and thinly sliced

4 to 6 Burger Buns (page 101), or store-bought

1 to 2 cups (250 to 500 ml) Garlic Herb Pizza + Pasta Sauce (page 173), or store-bought, warmed

½ cup (80 g) Vegan Parmesan (page 65), or store-bought

Preheat the oven to 325°F (163°C). Line a baking sheet with parchment paper.

To make the quinoa meatballs, in a small bowl, whisk together the ground flax and warm water. Set aside to gelatinize, about 5 minutes.

Meanwhile, heat the olive oil in a small frying pan over medium heat. Sauté the garlic until fragrant, 2 to 3 minutes. Keep the pan on the stove to fry the meatballs in.

Combine the flax mixture, sautéed garlic, cooked quinoa, fresh basil, fresh oregano, bread crumbs, chickpeas, salt and red pepper flakes in a food processor and pulse until a thick paste forms. Move the mixture to a bowl and heat the frying pan over medium heat again. Scoop 1½-inch (3.8-cm) balls into the frying pan and sauté until golden and crisp, 4 to 5 minutes. Move the cooked balls to the lined baking sheet. Repeat this process until all of the meatballs are cooked.

Place the baking sheet into the oven and bake for 15 minutes, to heat the balls all the way through.

While the meatballs bake, prepare the grilled onions and peppers by heating the olive oil in a large frying or cast-iron pan over medium heat. Sauté the onions and peppers together until softened, about 5 minutes. Remove from the heat.

When everything is ready, slice open the buns and stuff 3 or 4 meatballs inside. Top with grilled onions and peppers, warm tomato sauce and a generous sprinkle of the vegan Parmesan. Serve and enjoy!

Leftover meatballs will keep for up to 1 week in the fridge. They can also be frozen and will thaw very well.

SOUTHERN COMFORT BOWL WITH SWEET POTATOES, BLACK BEANS, CILANTRO LIME QUINOA, ONION RINGS + SPICY RANCH SAUCE

This is the ultimate comfort food bowl. It's packed with spicy Southern flavors and textures and, of course, protein! It's a hearty dish that ends with a fiery kick—I literally would take a bath in that spicy ranch sauce if I could! Sure, it takes a little time to prepare, but it is so worth it. Let's get cookin'!

SERVES 2

SWEET POTATOES

1 medium sweet potato

1 tsp olive oil

Pinch each of salt and pepper

BLACK BEANS

1 tbsp (15 ml) olive oil

1½ cups (100 g) cooked black beans

½ tsp salt

¼ tsp cayenne pepper

CILANTRO LIME QUINOA

½ cup (95 g) uncooked quinoa

1 cup (240 ml) water

1 tsp lime juice

1 tsp chopped fresh cilantro

SPICY RANCH SAUCE

½ cup (120 g) Eggless Mayo (page 178)

1 tbsp (15 ml) Homemade Nut Milk (page 177), or store-bought

1 tsp apple cider vinegar

1 tsp lemon juice

1 tsp chopped fresh parsley

1 tsp chopped fresh chives

1 tsp chopped fresh dill

¼ tsp salt

¼ tsp garlic powder

¼ tsp onion powder

¼ tsp cayenne pepper

⅛ tsp smoked paprika

1 batch Crispy Baked Onion Rings (page 89)

1 jalapeño, thinly sliced

Lime wedges and fresh cilantro, for garnish

To make the sweet potatoes, preheat the oven to 375°F (191°C) and line a baking sheet with parchment paper. Slice the sweet potato into ½-inch (13-mm) rounds and lay flat on the baking sheet. Drizzle with the olive oil and sprinkle with salt and pepper. Bake for 20 to 25 minutes, flipping halfway through.

To make the black beans, combine the olive oil, black beans, salt and cayenne pepper in a small saucepan and cook over low heat for 10 to 15 minutes, stirring occasionally, until completely heated through.

To make the cilantro lime quinoa, pour the quinoa and water in a medium-size pot. Bring to a boil, then reduce the heat and simmer for about 10 minutes, until the ends spiral out. Remove from the heat, stir in the lime juice and cilantro, and set aside.

To make the spicy ranch sauce, combine the mayo, nut milk, apple cider vinegar, lemon juice, parsley, chives, dill, salt, garlic powder, onion powder, cayenne pepper and smoked paprika in a food processor and pulse until creamy. Set aside.

Assemble the Southern Comfort Bowls by scooping the quinoa into two large bowls. Top with black beans, sweet potatoes, onion rings, spicy ranch sauce and sliced jalapeños. Garnish with lime wedges and freshly chopped cilantro and serve!

*See photo on page 50.

Tip

Read through ALL the directions before starting! There's a lot of prep involved and it helps to know what you should be doing before starting.

BUFFALO CAULIFLOWER BITES

Who needs chicken wings or processed faux meats when you can have these healthier, satisfying Buffalo Cauliflower Bites, instead? These babies pack a spicy punch and are a serious crowd-pleaser. They'll go quickly, so for bigger parties I suggest doubling the recipe!

SERVES 2 TO 4

1½ cups (360 ml) unsweetened almond milk

1 cup (125 g) all-purpose flour

2 tsp (6 g) garlic powder

1 tsp onion powder

1 tsp cumin

1 tsp smoked paprika

¼ tsp salt

¼ tsp pepper

1 large head cauliflower, cut into florets (about 6 cups [1.4 kg])

1 tbsp (15 g) vegan butter

1 cup (240 ml) Frank's RedHot sauce (see Tip)

Preheat the oven to 450°F (232°C). Line a baking sheet with parchment paper.

In a medium-size mixing bowl, whisk together the almond milk, flour, garlic powder, onion powder, cumin, smoked paprika, salt and pepper.

Dip the florets into the mixture, coating evenly. Tap off any excess batter and place the florets on the baking sheet. Bake for about 20 minutes, flipping halfway through.

While the cauliflower bites cook, heat the butter and hot sauce together in a small saucepan, stirring occasionally, until the butter just melts. When the cauliflower bites have cooked, pull them from the oven and, using tongs, carefully dip each floret completely into the hot sauce mixture and place it back on the baking sheet. Continue this until all the florets have been dipped. Bake for 25 to 30 more minutes, again flipping about halfway through.

When they're finished, serve immediately with vegan ranch dressing and sliced vegetables or just enjoy as is!

Tip

Frank's RedHot is a pretty mild, guest-friendly hot sauce. If you like it spicier, use your hot sauce of choice, instead!

HEIRLOOM TOMATO + HEMP GAZPACHO

If you're searching for a quick, easy meal that looks and tastes like you ordered out from a fancy restaurant, then you've come to the right place! This simple soup couldn't be easier—just chop and blend! It pulls together some of the best flavors of summer while keeping it light and simple, so you can spend less time in the kitchen and more time bragging about your kitchen skills.

SERVES 4

3 cups (635 g) quartered heirloom tomatoes

¾ cup (150 g) chopped red onion

¾ cup (150 g) chopped red bell pepper

½ cup (28 g) packed basil leaves, plus more for garnish

¼ cup (31 g) hemp seeds, plus more for garnish

1 clove garlic, minced

2 tbsp (30 ml) lemon juice

1 tbsp (15 ml) olive oil

1 tbsp (15 ml) balsamic vinegar

1 tsp salt

½ tsp ground pepper

Using a high-speed blender or an immersion blender, blend all of the ingredients together until smooth. Serve immediately in chilled glasses or bowls, garnished with hemp seeds and fresh basil.

If it heats up in the blender, just pop it in the fridge to chill before serving.

CAULIFLOWER STEAKS WITH PESTO + GRILLED ONIONS

These cauliflower steaks are super easy to make and look fancy to serve at a dinner party. The cauliflower steaks would be great on their own, but the salty pesto and savory grilled onions kick it up a notch for sure. They take an ordinary vegetable and turn it into a mouthwatering main dish. They'll go quick, so double the recipe for larger groups!

SERVES 2

CAULIFLOWER STEAKS

1 large head cauliflower, sliced into 1" to 1½" (2.5- to 3.8-cm) thick slices

1 tbsp (15 ml) olive oil

⅛ tsp salt

⅛ tsp pepper

GRILLED ONIONS

1 tbsp (15 ml) olive oil

2 medium sweet onions, thinly sliced

1 to 6 tbsp (15 to 90 ml) water, as needed

½ cup (260 g) Hemp Seed Basil Pesto (page 170), or store-bought

Micro greens or parsley, for garnish

Lemon slices, for garnish

To make the cauliflower steaks, preheat the oven to 400°F (205°C). Place the slices of cauliflower, the "steaks," on a parchment-lined baking sheet. Drizzle with the olive oil and sprinkle with the salt and pepper.

Bake the cauliflower steaks for 40 to 50 minutes, flipping halfway through. They are done when they are fork-tender but crispy on the outside.

While the cauliflower cooks, prepare the grilled onions. Heat the olive oil in a cast-iron skillet over medium-low heat. Sauté the onions for about 20 minutes, stirring occasionally and adding water as needed to prevent sticking. They should be a deep golden color when finished.

Plate the dish by topping the cauliflower steaks with the grilled onions and pesto. Garnish with micro greens and lemon slices before serving. Enjoy!

Tip

Make the pesto ahead to save time. You can make a batch and use it for a few different recipes!

LOBSTER MUSHROOM BISQUE

This recipe is totally fancy restaurant food. Your friends will think you called in and picked up an order of lobster stew, because how else could you have whipped up such a stunning, creamy, rich, velvety soup? Lobster mushrooms serve as the source of the salty, lobsterlike flavor and color behind this soup. They grow in the wild but are easily found dried online. They give off the aroma of the sea and make a perfect creamy bisque reminiscent of the seafood-based versions. The only thing that could make it better would be a sprinkle of oyster crackers!

SERVES 6

CASHEW CREAM

2 cups (480 ml) hot water

1 cup (150 g) cashews

1 cup (240 ml) water

BISQUE

4 tbsp (60 g) vegan butter

3 cloves garlic, minced

1 medium yellow onion, chopped

2 medium carrots, thinly sliced

2 medium celery stalks, thinly sliced

3 oz (85 g) dried lobster mushrooms or 1 lb (450 g) fresh lobster mushrooms

½ cup (120 ml) white cooking wine

2 tbsp (20 g) all-purpose flour

6 cups (1.4 L) vegetable broth

½ tsp salt

¼ tsp pepper

Fresh parsley, for garnish

To make the cashew cream, pour the hot water and cashews into a bowl and soak for at least 30 minutes. Drain the water. Pour the soaked cashews and 1 cup (240 ml) water into a blender and blend until creamy. Pour into a bowl and set aside.

To make the bisque, heat 1 tablespoon (15 g) of the vegan butter in a large soup pot or Dutch oven over medium heat. Sauté the garlic, onion, carrots, celery and mushrooms together until soft, 5 to 6 minutes. Deglaze the pan with the white wine and cook until the liquid reduces, 3 to 5 minutes.

Add the remaining 3 tablespoons (45 g) vegan butter and flour, stirring to combine. Cook for about 5 minutes, then pour in the vegetable broth, salt and pepper and simmer for 30 more minutes.

When the soup is ready, blend the soup with a high-speed or immersion blender until smooth. Pour in the cashew cream, stirring to combine. Serve garnished with fresh parsley!

Tip

Lobster mushrooms can be expensive. Buying them dried online is your best bet!

CAESAR SALAD WITH HOMEMADE DILL CROUTONS

I love a good Caesar salad! It's the perfect lunch or light dinner and tastes good anytime of the year. This dressing is as rich and salty as the original, but much better for you. The homemade dill croutons are tangy and crunchy, and the vegan Parmesan cheese takes the salad to a whole new level of delicious! This salad is the perfect excuse for working more greens into your diet and is a delicious, dairy-free alternative to the original.

SERVES 6

2 medium bunches romaine lettuce, chopped (about 8 cups [600 g])

1 medium bunch lacinato kale, stems removed, chopped (about 3 cups [200 g])

1 cup (50 g) thinly sliced scallions

DRESSING

½ cup (75 g) raw cashews

1 cup (240 ml) hot water

2 tbsp (30 ml) olive oil

1 tbsp (15 ml) lemon juice

2 tsp (18 g) Dijon mustard

3 cloves garlic

2 tbsp (14 g) nutritional yeast

½ tsp salt

½ tsp pepper

¼ cup (60 ml) water

DILL CROUTONS

6 cups (300 g) cubed stale sourdough bread (1" [2.5 cm] cubes)

3 tbsp (45 ml) olive oil

3 tbsp (9 g) chopped fresh dill

½ tsp salt

¼ tsp pepper

VEGAN PARMESAN

1 cup (150 g) raw cashews

¼ cup (28 g) nutritional yeast

¾ tsp salt

¼ tsp garlic powder

Preheat the oven to 375°F (191°C). Line a baking sheet with parchment paper.

Place the chopped greens and scallions in a large salad bowl and set aside in the fridge to chill.

To make the dressing, soak the raw cashews in the hot water for at least 30 minutes. Drain the water off and pour the cashews into a food processor or high-speed blender. Pour in the olive oil, lemon juice, Dijon, garlic cloves, nutritional yeast, salt, pepper and water and blend on high speed until the mixture becomes creamy. Pour the dressing into a small bowl and place it in the fridge to chill with the greens.

To make the croutons, spread the stale bread cubes over the lined baking sheet and drizzle evenly with the olive oil. Toss the cubes to evenly coat them in the oil, then sprinkle the fresh dill, salt and pepper over the top. Bake for 8 to 10 minutes, flipping halfway through. Set aside to cool.

While the croutons bake, prepare the vegan Parmesan by combining the cashews, nutritional yeast, salt and garlic powder in a food processor. Pulse until the mixture become a fine meal.

To prepare the Caesar salad, pull the greens from the fridge and drizzle with the dressing. You don't need to use it all, your choice. Use two spoons or a set of tongs to toss the greens evenly in the dressing. Sprinkle the croutons and Parmesan cheese generously over the top and serve immediately!

You may have leftover dressing and cheese. The dressing and cheese will both keep for up to 2 weeks in airtight containers in the refrigerator.

CAULIFLOWER RICE RISOTTO WITH HOMEMADE PARMESAN

I love this recipe because the cauliflower rice makes the dish taste so much lighter and healthier—but topped with my rich, homemade Parmesan cheese, you won't feel like you're missing a thing. It's creamy, much easier to make than it sounds and *perfect* for date night.

SERVES 2

CAULIFLOWER RICE RISOTTO

2 cups (450 g) cauliflower florets

1 tbsp (15 ml) olive oil

2 cloves garlic, minced

2 medium leeks, ends trimmed, thinly sliced

1 medium bulb fennel, ends trimmed, chopped

1 small red bell pepper, cored and chopped

4 tbsp (12 g) chopped fresh parsley, plus more for garnish

¼ cup (60 ml) dry white cooking wine

½ cup (120 ml) vegetable broth

⅛ tsp salt

½ cup (75 g) pine nuts

¼ cup (40 g) Vegan Parmesan (page 65)

To make the risotto, place the cauliflower in a food processor and pulse until it resembles the texture of rice. Set aside.

Heat the olive oil over medium heat in a large skillet. Sauté the garlic, leeks, fennel, bell pepper and parsley for 5 to 8 minutes, or until soft and fragrant. Deglaze the pan with the white wine, and cook, stirring, until the liquid mostly evaporates, about 5 minutes. Add the vegetable broth and salt and simmer for 5 more minutes. Blend about half of the mixture with an immersion blender, then pour it back into the pan. Stir in the cauliflower "rice" and pine nuts, and cook until heated through. Top with fresh parsley and vegan Parmesan, for garnish.

TANGY PURPLE CABBAGE SLAW WITH DIJON + HORSERADISH

An easy way to sneak more veggies into your diet? Make them taste incredible! This slaw packs a serious punch and a ton of flavor. The combination of sweet, spicy and tangy comes together in the best kind of way. It's great on its own, as a sandwich or burger topper, even in tacos! All you need is a little vegan mayo. Who knew vegetables could taste so good?

SERVES 4 TO 6

½ cup (120 g) Eggless Mayo (page 178), or store-bought

1 small clove garlic, minced

1 tbsp (16 g) whole-grain Dijon mustard

1½ tsp (7 ml) apple cider vinegar

1½ tsp (3 g) finely grated fresh horseradish

½ tsp sugar

¼ tsp salt

¼ tsp pepper

4 cups (400 g) shredded purple cabbage

In a large mixing bowl, whisk together the vegan mayo, garlic, Dijon mustard, apple cider vinegar, horseradish, sugar, salt and pepper. Pour in the shredded cabbage and toss to coat evenly. Serve immediately!

Leftovers will keep for about 4 days in the fridge.

TUNA-LESS SALAD SANDWICH

I've always loved a good tuna sandwich, but I prefer this version much more—it's packed with protein from the chickpeas, is lighter with eggless mayo and has a ton of flavor. It's perfect for taking to work for lunch or bringing along on a picnic, and somehow tastes *even better* after sitting in the fridge for a day.

SERVES 2

2 cups (400 g) cooked chickpeas

¼ cup (57 g) Eggless Mayo (page 178), or store-bought

¼ cup (40 g) finely chopped red onion

¼ cup (37 g) thinly sliced celery

1 tbsp (15 ml) lemon juice

1 tsp Dijon mustard

1 tsp chopped fresh dill

1 tsp celery seed

½ tsp Old Bay seasoning

¼ tsp pepper

⅛ tsp salt

Pour the chickpeas into a large bowl and use a fork to mash about half of them. Add the rest of the ingredients and use a wooden spoon to toss and combine them. Serve over greens, on bread or enjoy as is!

chapter four

CROWD-PLEASERS

The best party food is dippable, snackable and tastes just as good before you've started drinking as it does after. Each of these crowd-pleasing recipes is easy to whip up and uses minimal dishes, so you can spend more time hanging banners with your friends and filtering Instagram photos and less time stuck in the kitchen. With dishes like Jalapeño Cornbread (page 85), Cheesy Spinach Artichoke Dip (page 86) and Buffalo Cauliflower Pizza with Ranch Sauce (page 74), I've got a dish for just about every occasion so you'll be the hostess with the mostest at your next gathering!

BUFFALO CAULIFLOWER PIZZA WITH RANCH SAUCE

Much like the Buffalo Cauliflower Bites (page 57) themselves, this pizza is a serious crowd-pleaser. It's packed with flavor and texture and is definitely one of my favorite recipes in this book. It comes together pretty easily and proves that you don't need meat to make a pizza taste incredible. It's about to become your new favorite pie!

SERVES 4

PIZZA

1 batch Perfect Pizza Dough (page 169), or store-bought

¼ cup (60 ml) Garlic Herb Pizza + Pasta Sauce (page 173)

½ cup (60 g) vegan cheese

2 medium celery stalks, thinly sliced

½ medium red onion, thinly sliced

½ recipe Buffalo Cauliflower Bites (page 57)

Chopped fresh parsley, for garnish

RANCH SAUCE

½ cup (120 g) Eggless Mayo (page 178), or store-bought

1 tbsp (15 ml) unsweetened almond milk

1 tsp apple cider vinegar

1 tsp lemon juice

1 tsp chopped fresh parsley

1 tsp chopped fresh chives

1 tsp chopped fresh dill

¼ tsp salt

¼ tsp garlic powder

¼ tsp onion powder

To make the pizza, preheat the oven to 500°F (260°C). Lightly flour a pizza stone or grease a pan. You can also just use a baking sheet, if that's all you've got on hand.

Roll or toss your dough into a large, thin pizza shape and spread over your prepared pizza pan.

Top evenly with the tomato sauce and vegan cheese. Sprinkle the celery and onion over the top, followed by the cauliflower bites. Bake for 7 to 12 minutes, until the edges are crisp and the cheese is melted.

While the pizza bakes, prepare the ranch sauce by combining the mayo, almond milk, vinegar, lemon juice, parsley, chives, dill, salt, garlic powder and onion powder in a food processor until creamy.

When the pizza is finished, pull it from the oven, drizzle the ranch sauce evenly over the top, and sprinkle with fresh parsley. Slice into 8 equal slices using a pizza cutter, and serve immediately!

Tip

A super hot oven is the key to making a perfect pizza. It doesn't overcook the toppings but makes the crust nice and crispy!

SOUTHERN FRIED ZUCCHINI FRITTERS

These fritters are easy to make, and they taste GREAT with beer! They're also kind of great for breakfast smothered in hot sauce alongside some roasted potatoes and avocado. Sure, they're fried, but why not splurge a little for a DELICIOUS meal? They're made of veggies, anyway! You won't regret it.

MAKES 8 LARGE FRITTERS

3 tbsp (18 g) chia seeds

½ cup (120 ml) warm water

½ cup (60 g) grated red onion

1 cup (160 g) grated carrots

1 cup (180 g) grated potatoes

2 cups (240 g) grated zucchini

½ cup (60 g) coconut oil, for frying

2 cloves garlic, minced

¼ cup (40 g) all-purpose flour

½ tsp baking powder

½ tsp cayenne

½ tsp smoked paprika

½ tsp salt

¼ tsp pepper

⅛ tsp cornstarch

Fresh cilantro, for garnish

Limes, for garnish

Hot sauce, for serving (optional)

Blend together the chia seeds and warm water in a high-speed blender or food processor and pour into a small bowl. Set aside.

Place the grated onion, carrots, potatoes and zucchini in a large colander and drain over the sink for about 5 minutes, using a paper towel to gently squeeze out any excess water.

Meanwhile, heat the coconut oil in a large cast-iron or frying pan over medium heat. Oil that isn't hot enough won't cook the fritter well, and oil that is too hot will burn it. Aim for the oil to be between 325°F and 400°F (163°C and 205°C), if you have a thermometer. Also, if you plan on subbing out a different oil for the coconut oil, make sure it too has a high smoke point or your pan will smoke and burn and ruin the taste of the fritter.

Once the veggies have drained as much excess liquid as possible, transfer them to a large mixing bowl. Add the blended chia mixture and garlic, stirring to combine. Next add in the flour, baking powder, cayenne, smoked paprika, salt, pepper and cornstarch and mix until completely combined.

Scoop ¼-cup (60-g) amounts of the mixture into the heated oil and press gently with the back of a spoon to flatten. Let cook for 2 to 3 minutes, until golden brown, before flipping and cooking several more minutes. Once the fritter is crispy and golden, use a spatula to move it to a paper towel-lined plate, which will help absorb any excess oil.

Serve immediately with some fresh cilantro, fresh lime and hot sauce, if you're into it. Freeze leftovers or refrigerate for up to 3 days.

PILE O' POUTINE

Poutine the perfect party food. Put out a huge tray of baked French fries covered in gravy and melty cheese and you will definitely be a hit of a hostess! This dish is more traditionally Canadian, but being that I grew up in Maine, and Vancouver has become my and my partner's favorite city to travel to, we've jumped on the poutine train, too. I simply sub my homemade cashew curds for the traditional mozzarella version and bake the fries instead of actually frying them. You can absolutely use my cheese recipe, or use what you have on hand. Traditionally poutine is made with "squeaky cheese" or cheese curds, but really melted cheese and gravy together of any sort are amazing. It is just SO good! And so easy. Go preheat the oven!

SERVES 4

2 lbs (970 g) russet potatoes, cut into ½" (13 mm) fries

2 tbsp (30 ml) olive oil

1 tsp salt

½ cup (120 g) Easy Cashew Cheese (page 174), or store-bought

GRAVY

2 tbsp (26 g) vegan butter

¼ cup (40 g) all-purpose flour

2 cups (480 ml) vegetable broth

½ tsp truffle or sea salt, or sub miso paste

¼ tsp onion powder

¼ tsp garlic powder

Fresh parsley, for garnish

Preheat oven to 425°F (218°C).

Spread sliced potatoes onto a tin foil-lined baking sheet. Drizzle with olive oil and sprinkle with salt, then bake for about 30 minutes, flipping the fries halfway through.

While the fries bake, prepare the gravy by melting the butter in a small saucepan over medium heat. Add the flour and cook about 5 minutes, until the flour has browned, to create a roux. Whisk in the vegetable broth, salt or miso paste, onion powder and garlic powder. Bring the mixture to a boil, then simmer for about 10 minutes, whisking occasionally, until the mixture thickens.

When the fries are ready, move them to a serving dish. Sprinkle the cheese all over and drizzle the gravy generously over the top. Serve with a bit of fresh parsley.

Tip

The fries can be sliced up the night before and left soaking in water until you're ready to bake them. This will result in a moister middle and crispier on the outside French fry.

MINI POLENTA PIZZAS

Making pizza is great but can be time-consuming, and sometimes you just don't have the energy to make your own dough at the end of a long day. Instead, you can make these easy-peasy personal pizzas for everyone—even the gluten-free foodies—at the party! They're fun to make and you can cover them in whatever toppings you like. Plus, they're portable. All you need is a little vegan cheese, and you're on your way!

MAKES 10 TO 12

3 cups (720 ml) water

1 tsp salt

1½ cups (290 g) uncooked polenta (corn grits)

½ cup (120 ml) Garlic Herb Pizza + Pasta Sauce (page 173), or store-bought

Assorted toppings (I use bell peppers, red onions and red pepper flakes)

1 cup (140 g) vegan cheese

Line two separate baking sheets with parchment paper and set aside.

Bring the water and salt to a boil in a large pot or Dutch oven. Pour in the polenta and stir to combine. Cook over low heat, stirring occasionally, until the mixture thickens and begins to pull away from the sides of the pot, about 5 minutes.

Remove the pot from the heat and pour the mixture onto one of the lined baking sheets, using a rubber spatula to spread it out to about ½-inch (13-mm) thick. Let cool on the counter for at least 30 minutes, until the polenta becomes solid and cools completely. While cooling, preheat the oven to 400°F (205°C).

Once cool, use a round cookie cutter or the open end of a drinking glass to cut rounds out of the polenta. Place the rounds onto the second lined baking sheet and bake for about 5 minutes on each side, to firm up the polenta "crust."

Pull the pan from the oven and spread a little tomato sauce onto each round. Sprinkle with the assorted toppings and vegan cheese and bake for 15 to 20 minutes, or until the cheese is melty and the pizzas are hot. Serve and enjoy!

SMOKY POTATO SALAD

I brought this to a girls' night get-together with my friends and it was a TOTAL HIT! And this was *before* we broke out the wine. It's smoky, a little spicy and super flavorful, more than you'd expect from a simple potato salad! It whips up quickly and serves plenty—the definition of perfect party food.

SERVES 6 TO 8

6 cups (1.4 kg) cubed red potatoes (1" [2.5 cm] cubes)

Pinch of salt

1 cup (165 g) diced celery

1 cup (170 g) diced red onion

½ cup (80 g) diced radishes

1¼ cups (300 g) Eggless Mayo (page 178), or store-bought

1 tbsp (15 ml) apple cider vinegar

1 tbsp (15 ml) lemon juice

2 tbsp (6 g) chopped fresh dill, plus more for garnish

1 clove garlic, minced

1 tsp smoked paprika

½ tsp cayenne pepper

½ tsp salt

½ tsp pepper

Pour the potatoes into a large soup pot. Add the salt and enough water to just cover the potatoes. Bring to a boil and cook for about 20 minutes, or until the potatoes are fork-tender. Drain the water and set aside to cool.

While the potatoes cool, prep the veggies and place them into a large bowl. Set those aside, too.

In a smaller bowl, whisk together the mayo, cider vinegar, lemon juice, fresh dill, garlic, smoked paprika, cayenne pepper, salt and pepper. Pour into the veggies and toss to combine.

When the potatoes have cooled completely, toss them in the veggie-mayo mixture until completely combined. Garnish with fresh dill and serve!

Leftovers will keep in the fridge for up to 1 week.

JALAPEÑO CORNBREAD

The perfect addition to just about any meal, this cornbread comes together quickly and packs a spicy punch. It's perfectly fluffy without the eggs, and I love it smothered in vegan butter or dipped into a big, hearty bowl of chili!

SERVES 8

1½ cups (180 g) yellow cornmeal

1½ cups (185 g) all-purpose flour

3 tbsp (43 g) sugar

1 tbsp (9 g) baking powder

½ tsp salt

1¾ cups (420 ml) cold, unsweetened almond milk

½ cup (90 g) diced jalapeños

Preheat the oven to 350°F (175°C). Grease or line a 9 x 13-inch (23 x 33-cm) baking dish.

In a large mixing bowl, whisk together the cornmeal, flour, sugar, baking powder and salt. Pour in the milk and jalapeños and whisk until just combined.

Pour the batter into the prepared baking dish and bake for 45 to 50 minutes, until the top begins to crack and an inserted toothpick comes out clean. Let cool for at least 5 minutes before slicing and serving.

Leftovers can be stored in an airtight container on the counter or in the fridge for up to 3 days.

CHEESY SPINACH ARTICHOKE DIP

I worked at a brew pub in high school that made the BEST spinach artichoke dip. Cheesy and rich, it was my favorite dish on the menu. These days, I prefer something dairy-free and way healthier—and this yummy appetizer does just the trick! It's just as cheesy, ooey-gooey and flavorful as the original, but totally guilt-free. Perfect for parties!

SERVES 6

1 heaping cup (245 g) cooked white beans

3 tbsp (18 g) nutritional yeast

¼ cup (60 ml) water

2 tsp (3 g) chopped fresh basil

1 tsp salt

1 tsp crushed red pepper

1 tbsp (15 ml) olive oil

6 cloves garlic, minced

1 large yellow onion, chopped

1 (14-oz [400-g]) can artichoke hearts, drained and chopped

4 cups (280 g) fresh spinach

¼ cup (35 g) Easy Cashew Cheese (page 174)

1 cup (120 g) bread crumbs

Preheat the oven to 400°F (205°C).

In a food processor, combine the white beans, nutritional yeast, water, fresh basil, salt and crushed red pepper until smooth. Scoop the mixture into a bowl and set aside.

In a medium cast-iron pan, heat the olive oil over medium heat. Sauté the garlic and onions together for 3 to 5 minutes, until softened. Pour in the chopped artichokes and stir to combine. Pour in the spinach, about a cup (70 g) at a time, stirring to wilt. When the spinach has wilted, shut off the heat and pour in the white bean mixture, vegan cheese and about three-fourths of the bread crumbs. Stir to combine completely.

Pour the remaining bread crumbs over the top of the mixture, then cover the pan with aluminum foil. Bake for 20 minutes. Remove the foil and bake for another 10 to 15 minutes, until the mixture is bubbly and hot. Let cool for 5 minutes, then serve with bread, chips or sliced vegetables!

Tip

If after you've added the cheese and bread crumbs you'd like to scoop the mixture into a different oven-safe baking dish, go for it, but adjust the cooking time accordingly.

CRISPY BAKED ONION RINGS

I always used to classify people in two ways: either you're a French fry person or you're an onion ring person. I've always considered myself an onion ringer, and the first time I made these baked onion rings, I couldn't believe how good they were! Just as crispy crunchy as the originals, but baked, way healthier and completely oil-free. This recipe will turn any French fry lover into an onion ringer, guaranteed!

SERVES 2 TO 4

1 large sweet onion

WET DIP

1 cup (125 g) all-purpose flour

3 tbsp (28 g) cornstarch

1¼ cups (300 ml) unsweetened almond milk

DRY DIP

1¼ cups (125 g) panko bread crumbs

½ cup (60 g) cornmeal

¼ cup (28 g) nutritional yeast

1 tsp salt

1 tsp garlic powder

½ tsp dried oregano

½ tsp smoked paprika

Preheat the oven to 425°F (218°C) and line a baking sheet with parchment paper.

Slice the large sweet onion into ½- to ¾-inch (13- to 19-mm) rings and set aside.

To make the wet dip, in a small bowl, whisk together the flour and cornstarch. Whisk in the almond milk until a smooth batter forms.

To make the dry dip, in a separate large bowl, combine the bread crumbs, cornmeal, nutritional yeast, salt, garlic powder, dried oregano and smoked paprika.

Dip the onion rings one at a time into the wet mixture, shaking off the excess, then dip them into the dry mixture, being sure to evenly coat the onion ring. Move the coated rings to the baking sheet. Continue until all the rings have been coated.

Bake the onion rings for 20 minutes, flipping halfway through. Serve with your favorite dip—I go with ketchup—and enjoy immediately!

Tip

Sub regular bread crumbs for the panko ones if you like, though the rings won't be quite as crunchy.

POTATO LEEK CROSTINI

These easy crostini whip up quickly and taste great—they're the perfect holiday party appetizer, no meat or dairy needed. The potato leek combo topped with fresh dill is out of this world, so make sure you have plenty for your guests!

SERVES 6 TO 8

1 sourdough or French bread baguette, sliced 1" (2.5 cm) thick

6 cups (1.4 L) water

1 lb (475 g) red potatoes, cut into 1" (2.5 cm) cubes

2 medium leeks, ends trimmed

2 cloves garlic

½ cup (115 g) Eggless Mayo (page 178) or store-bought

2 tsp (10 ml) apple cider vinegar

2 tsp (10 ml) lemon juice

1½ tsp (3 g) chopped fresh dill, plus more for garnish

½ teaspoon salt

¼ teaspoon pepper

Preheat the oven to 400°F (205°C). Line a baking sheet with parchment paper.

Spread the bread slices on the baking sheet and bake for 10 to 20 minutes, flipping halfway through, until they're golden and crisp. Set aside to cool.

In a medium-size pot, combine the water and cubed red potatoes. Bring to a low boil for about 20 minutes, or until the potatoes are fork-tender. Drain the water and set aside.

Thinly slice the leeks and mince the garlic. Set aside.

In a medium-size mixing bowl, whisk together the mayo, apple cider vinegar, lemon juice, fresh dill, salt and pepper. Add in the leeks, garlic and cooled potatoes and toss to evenly coat them in the sauce mixture.

Scoop the mixture onto the slices of baguette and top with a sprinkle of fresh dill. Serve and enjoy!

Tip
You can easily make the potato leek mixture ahead and just use when you're ready. I would NOT recommend baking the slices of baguette until you're ready to eat them or they'll get too hard.

BAKED SEA SALTED SOFT PRETZELS WITH SPICY MUSTARD DIP

There's nothing that takes me back to childhood like a giant, salted soft pretzel. Sitting at baseball games with my dad as a kid, I always had a pretzel bigger than my head. It's what sports are all about for me—the food! This recipe was easily made vegan and is perfect for serving at a Super Bowl or Stanley Cup party, or just for making and eating all by yourself—I won't judge!

MAKES 8

PRETZELS

1½ cups (360 ml) warm water
(at 110°F to 115°F [43°C to 46°C])

1 tbsp (14 g) sugar

2 tsp (10 g) salt

2¼ tsp (7 g) active dry yeast

2¼ tsp (60 ml) vegan butter, melted

4¼ cups (530 g) all-purpose flour

10 cups (2.4 L) plus ½ cup (120 ml) water, divided

⅔ cup (137 g) baking soda

1 tbsp (9 g) cornstarch

Large-grain sea salt, for sprinkling

MUSTARD DIP

½ cup (136 g) Dijon mustard

2 tbsp (30 ml) maple syrup

To make the pretzels, combine the water, sugar and salt in the bowl of a stand mixer. Sprinkle the yeast on top and let sit for about 5 minutes, until it begins to foam. Add the butter and flour and, using the dough hook attachment, mix on low speed until well combined. Change to medium speed and let the hook knead the mixture until it is smooth and pulls away from the sides of the bowl, 3 to 5 minutes.

Remove the dough from the bowl, wipe it out, and use a paper towel to generously grease the inside. Place the dough back inside the bowl and cover with plastic wrap or a clean dish towel. Leave the bowl in a warm place for 50 to 60 minutes, or until the dough has doubled in size.

Preheat the oven to 450°F (232°C). Line a baking sheet with parchment paper and set aside. Bring 10 cups (2.4 L) of the water and the baking soda to a rolling boil in a large pot or Dutch oven. In a small dish, whisk together the remaining ½ cup (120 ml) water and cornstarch.

While the oven preheats and the water comes to a boil, turn out the dough onto a lightly floured work surface and divide into 8 equal pieces. Roll each piece of dough into about a 24-inch (61-cm) rope. Holding the ends of the rope, make a U-shape with the rope and cross the ends, pressing them into the bottom of the U-shape to make a pretzel shape. (Or just make whatever shapes you like!) Set the formed pretzels to the side until each pretzel is laid out.

One by one, place the pretzels into the boiling water for about 30 seconds. Use a slotted spoon to remove them from the water and place them onto the prepared baking sheet. Continue this process until all of the pretzels have been boiled and are laid on the baking sheet. Brush the top of each pretzel with the water and cornstarch mixture and sprinkle with a bit of sea salt. Bake the pretzels for 12 to 14 minutes, until they are a dark golden brown color. Move them to a cooling rack to cool slightly before serving.

To prepare the mustard dip, simply mix together the Dijon mustard and maple syrup. Serve alongside the warm pretzels!

Leftover pretzels keep well in an airtight container on the counter for 3 days.

chapter five

COOK UP SOME COMFORT FOOD

Whether it's cold outside and you've got nowhere to go or you've just been through a hell of a breakup, knowing how to cook up good comfort food is a necessity. Dishes like my Baked Butternut Squash Mac 'n' Cheese (page 96), Chickpea Noodle Soup (page 99) and Creamy Corn Chowder (page 109) will have you feeling better in no time. This is the first place to go when you're craving a big bowl of goodness, a hug in the form of food. I took some of Grandma's traditional recipes, added a bunch of hidden plant goodness and served them up here for you to enjoy. I just know you're gonna love 'em!

BAKED BUTTERNUT SQUASH MAC 'N' CHEESE

My mom made a mean baked mac 'n' cheese when I was a kid. Cheesy, ooey-gooey and covered in crispy bread crumbs—it was one of my favorite meals! This butternut squash version blends the sweet and savory flavors of winter squash into a cheesy sauce to make a meal that'll totally take you back to childhood. I covered mine in bread crumbs, too. Mom would be proud!

SERVES 6 TO 8

6 cups (840 g) peeled and cubed butternut squash (1" [2.5 cm] cubes)

1 tbsp (15 ml) olive oil

Salt and pepper

1 lb (454 g) elbow noodles

1½ cups (360 ml) unsweetened almond milk

⅔ cup (80 g) nutritional yeast

3 tbsp (45 ml) lemon juice

1 tbsp (14 g) Dijon mustard

1 clove garlic

½ tsp turmeric

⅓ cup (50 g) bread crumbs

Fresh parsley, for garnish

Preheat the oven to 400°F (205°C). Line a baking sheet with parchment paper.

Spread the cubed squash onto the baking sheet. Drizzle with the olive oil, sprinkle with salt and pepper and bake for about 30 minutes, flipping halfway through, until fork-tender. Keep the oven on.

While the squash roasts, bring a medium pot of water to a boil. Pour in the elbow noodles and a pinch of salt and bring back to a boil. Cook for 6 to 10 minutes, until al dente. Strain and set aside.

When the squash is ready, pour it into a high-speed blender or food processor along with the almond milk, nutritional yeast, lemon juice, Dijon mustard, garlic, turmeric and 1 teaspoon each salt and pepper. Blend until smooth, then pour the mixture over the cooked noodles and stir to combine.

Pour the mixture into a 9 x 13-inch (23 x 33-cm) baking dish, top with the bread crumbs and bake for about 15 minutes, or until the mixture is bubbling and golden. Serve with a sprinkle of fresh parsley!

Tip

Creamier mac more your style? Skip the baking!

CHICKPEA NOODLE SOUP

Whether you're sick with a fever or a broken heart, this soup is the answer. I've replaced the chicken in this classic comfort food with chickpeas to give you the protein you need to help recover, and the broth filled with fresh thyme and garlic will smell so good your sinuses will want to clear up all on their own! If you're still heartbroken, a little ice cream probably wouldn't hurt either.

SERVES 6

2 tbsp (30 ml) olive oil

4 cloves garlic, minced

2 medium onions, chopped

4 medium carrots, thinly sliced

4 celery stalks, thinly sliced

6 to 8 sprigs fresh thyme

1 bay leaf

2 quarts (2 L) vegetable broth

8 oz (227 g) whole wheat rotini noodles

1 cup (200 g) cooked chickpeas

Salt and pepper to taste

Chopped fresh parsley, for garnish

Crackers or bread, for garnish

In a cast-iron Dutch oven or large soup pot, heat the olive oil over medium heat. Add the garlic, onions, carrots, celery, fresh thyme and bay leaf and sauté until the veggies are softened, but not browned.

Add the vegetable broth and bring to a boil.

Once the soup is boiling, add the noodles and chickpeas and cook for about 8 minutes, until the noodles are almost completely cooked (don't worry, they'll continue cooking in the water). Add salt and pepper to taste.

Remove from the heat and serve with freshly chopped parsley and salty crackers or bread.

Leftover soup can be refrigerated for up to 1 week or frozen indefinitely and reheated as needed.

Tip
You can sub gluten-free noodles here, if you prefer!

BISCUITS WITH MUSHROOM GRAVY

I used to have biscuits and gravy EVERY Christmas morning growing up. Of course, it wasn't plant-based or very good for you, but it was delicious. This version is way healthier, has tons of great mushroom flavor and is the perfect replacement for the biscuits and gravy I grew up eating. The biscuits are fluffy, the gravy is savory and they make a fantastic combination!

SERVES 4 TO 8

1 batch Fluffy Whole Wheat Biscuits (page 166)

MUSHROOM GRAVY

3 tbsp (45 g) vegan butter, divided

2 cloves garlic, minced

1 medium yellow onion, chopped small

8 oz (227 g) cremini mushrooms, chopped small

3 or 4 sprigs fresh thyme, plus more for garnish

Salt and pepper

¼ cup (30 g) all-purpose flour

2 cups (480 ml) vegetable broth

1 tsp miso paste

Snipped chives, for garnish

Preheat the oven to 200°F (93°C) and place the biscuits in the oven to warm while you make the gravy. (You can skip this step if you don't want your biscuits warmed!)

To make the mushroom gravy, melt 1 tablespoon (15 g) of the butter over medium heat in a large frying pan. Sauté the garlic and onions together until softened and fragrant, about 3 minutes. Add the mushrooms, thyme and a pinch each of salt and pepper and continue to sauté for about 5 more minutes, until the mushrooms are softened. Turn off the heat, toss the thyme stems in the compost or trash, and set the pan aside.

In a large saucepan, melt the remaining 2 tablespoons (30 g) butter over medium-low heat. Pour in the flour and stir to create a roux. Let the roux cook for about 8 minutes, stirring occasionally so it doesn't stick or burn, but browns.

Whisk in the vegetable broth, miso paste and ¼ teaspoon pepper until completely combined. Continue cooking the mixture over medium heat until it comes to a boil. Reduce the heat, pour in the mushroom mixture and simmer until the gravy thickens, stirring occasionally, 10 to 15 minutes.

Pour the gravy over the biscuits and serve with a sprinkle of fresh thyme and chives.

Leftover gravy will keep for up to 1 week in an airtight container in the fridge.

*See photo on page 94.

Tip
You can make the biscuits up to 2 days before making the gravy, as long as you keep the biscuits in an airtight container.

SLOPPY CHICKS

These sloppy chicks are the much healthier, better-for-you version of traditional sloppy Joes! Made with chickpeas, they're packed with protein and super hearty—the perfect weeknight meal. I made my own buns here and will show you how, too, but you can sub in store-bought buns to make it even easier. Either way, these sloppy chicks are the kind you'll want more of in your kitchen!

SERVES 6

BURGER BUNS

3 cups (375 g) all-purpose flour

2 tbsp (24 g) sugar

2¼ tsp (7 g) active dry yeast

1 tsp salt

1 cup (240 ml) unsweetened almond milk, at room temperature, plus more for brushing

3 tbsp (45 ml) coconut oil, melted

Sesame seeds, for sprinkling (optional)

SLOPPY CHICKS

1 tsp coconut or olive oil

3 cloves garlic, minced

1 medium yellow onion, chopped

2 medium red bell peppers, cored and chopped

2 medium tomatoes, chopped

2 tbsp (30 ml) soy sauce or coconut aminos

2 tbsp (30 ml) Sriracha

1 tbsp (15 ml) maple syrup

1 tsp liquid smoke

2 tbsp (12 g) cumin

1 tbsp (9 g) nutritional yeast

1 tbsp (3 g) finely chopped fresh thyme

½ tsp smoked paprika

½ tsp dried oregano

½ tsp salt

½ tsp pepper

3 cups (600 g) cooked chickpeas, half mashed with a fork and set aside

Pickles, for garnish

(continued)

SLOPPY CHICKS (CONTINUED)

Preheat the oven to 400°F (205°C). Line a baking sheet with parchment paper.

To make the buns, in the bowl of a stand mixer, whisk together the flour, sugar, yeast and salt. Add the unsweetened almond milk and melted coconut oil and beat until the dough comes together. Switch to the dough hook and knead for about 5 minutes on medium speed, until the dough is smooth. If the dough is too sticky, you can add a bit more flour as needed.

Turn out the dough onto a lightly floured surface and shape it into a log. Cover it with a clean, slightly damp dish towel and let sit for 15 minutes.

Divide the dough into 6 equal pieces, and form each piece into a ball. For hamburger buns, flatten the balls into 3½-inch (9-cm) disks. (For hot dog buns, shape the dough balls into 4½-inch [11.4-cm] logs, instead.) Place the disks onto the prepared baking sheet about 1 inch (2.5 cm) apart. Let them rise near the oven for 20 minutes. Lightly brush the tops with almond milk and sprinkle with sesame seeds, if using.

Bake for about 15 minutes, or until golden brown. Let the buns cool completely on a wire rack before slicing horizontally. Set aside.

To make the sloppy chicks, in a large cast-iron or frying pan, heat the oil and sauté the garlic, onion and peppers until softened, about 5 minutes. Add in the tomatoes and cook 2 to 3 more minutes. Pour in the soy sauce, Sriracha, maple syrup, liquid smoke, cumin, nutritional yeast, thyme, smoked paprika, oregano, salt, pepper and chickpeas. Simmer for 15 minutes, stirring occasionally.

Serve on the sliced buns with pickles!

FRENCH ONION SOUP

I'd never been a huge fan of French onion soup until recently. I've always been lactose intolerant, so melty cheese–covered soup wasn't really my style. My partner, Alex, however, has been to Paris and had the *real* version, so I knew I had a great recipe tester for this soup—and I really wanted to impress him! The verdict? He LOVED it. He didn't think he'd ever be able to have the real thing again! This recipe will be a staple in our kitchen for years to come.

SERVES 4 TO 6

¼ cup (60 g) vegan butter

3 cloves garlic, mined

4 large yellow onions, thinly sliced (about 3 lb [1.4 kg])

2 bay leaves

2 sprigs fresh thyme

½ tsp salt

2 tbsp (18 g) all-purpose flour

¾ cup (180 ml) dry white wine

6 cups (1.4 L) vegetable broth

1 crusty baguette, sliced

1 to 2 cups (150 to 300 g) shredded Easy Cashew Cheese (page 174), for melting

Fresh parsley, for garnish

Heat the butter over medium-low heat in large Dutch oven. Sauté the garlic and onions along with the bay leaves, fresh thyme and salt for 50 to 60 minutes, stirring occasionally, until the onions are caramelized and soft.

Stir in the flour and cook for 2 minutes, then deglaze the pan with the white wine. Cook for about 2 more minutes, then pour in the vegetable broth. Simmer for 30 minutes, stirring occasionally.

While the soup cooks, set the oven to broil. Lay the baguette slices on a parchment-lined baking sheet and broil for a few minutes on each side, until the bread is golden and crisp. Set aside, but leave the broiler on.

When the soup has finished, toss the bay leaves and thyme stems out and pour servings of the soup into oven-safe crocks or bowls. Top with a slice or two of crusty baguette, then add a generous sprinkle of vegan cheese. Place the crocks under the broiler for several minutes, until the cheese is melty and bubbling. Serve immediately with a sprinkle of fresh parsley!

Leftover soup will keep in an airtight container in the fridge for up to 1 week.

Tip

The soup can easily be made ahead and refrigerated until you're ready to dish it into crocks and broil it.

COTTAGE PIE

This Cottage Pie is my healthier, yummier version of a traditional shepard's pie. Instead of ground beef, I used lentils for the protein! This recipe has a ton of flavor and surprised me when I was making it—I liked it WAY more than I ever expected! This would make a great weeknight meal with leftovers and is the perfect casserole for sharing with friends and family.

SERVES 8

POTATOES

2½ lb (1.1 kg) red potatoes, halved

Salt and pepper

2 tbsp (30 g) vegan butter

2 to 4 tbsp (30 to 60 ml) unsweetened almond milk

FILLING

1 tbsp (15 ml) olive oil

2 cloves garlic, minced

1 cup (150 g) chopped yellow onion

2 cups (300 g) mixed frozen corn, peas and carrots (or sub fresh!)

2 cups (350 g) cooked green or brown lentils

3 cups (720 ml) vegetable broth

1 tbsp (15 ml) soy sauce or coconut aminos

2 tsp (3 g) chopped fresh thyme

1 tsp salt

½ tsp pepper

2 tbsp (12 g) cornstarch

Fresh parsley, for garnish

To make the potatoes, in a large pot, place the halved red potatoes and ⅛ teaspoon salt. Add enough water to just cover the potatoes, and cook over medium heat for 20 to 30 minutes, until fork-tender. Remove from the heat, drain the water and add in the vegan butter, unsweetened almond milk (as needed), and salt and pepper to taste. Mash the mixture with a potato masher until fluffy. Set aside.

To make the filling, in a large frying or cast-iron pan, heat the olive oil over medium heat. Sauté the garlic and onions for 3 to 5 minutes, until softened. Add in the frozen mixed vegetables, lentils, vegetable broth, soy sauce, fresh thyme, salt and pepper. Whisk in the cornstarch and continue cooking over medium heat until the mixture comes to a boil.

Reduce the heat and simmer for about 10 minutes, stirring occasionally, until the mixture has thickened. Remove from the heat and preheat the oven to 350°F (175°C).

Pour the vegetable mixture into a 9 x 13-inch (23 x 33-cm) baking dish. Scoop the mashed potatoes over the top and spread them evenly over the mixture using a fork or the back of a wooden spoon. Poke a few holes in the potato mixture with the fork or a toothpick, so steam can escape while cooking.

Bake for 25 to 30 minutes, or until the potatoes are golden on top. Sprinkle with fresh parsley and serve immediately!

Leftovers keep well in the fridge for up to 1 week.

CREAMY CORN CHOWDER

Maine—where I grew up—is famous for its creamy seafood-based chowders, but I always preferred the lighter, smokier flavor of a simple corn chowder. This version is easy, tastes great and is hearty enough to fill you up. Best served with salty crackers or crusty bread!

SERVES 6

1 tbsp (15 ml) olive oil

3 cloves garlic, minced

1 large yellow onion, chopped

2 red bell peppers, cored and chopped

3 celery stalks, thinly sliced

2 medium Yukon gold potatoes, cut into ½" (13-mm) cubes

5 ears corn, husked

¾ tsp smoked paprika

¾ tsp salt

¾ tsp pepper

1 (14-oz [414-ml]) can full-fat coconut milk

2 cups (480 ml) vegetable broth

Fresh parsley, for garnish

Heat the olive oil in a large soup pot or Dutch oven over medium heat. Add the garlic and onion and sauté for 2 to 3 minutes, until fragrant.

Add the bell peppers, celery and potatoes and stir to combine. Use a knife to carefully slice the corn kernels off the cob and add them to the pot as well. (If you'd like to garnish the soup like I did, simply set aside about 2 tablespoons [30 g] uncooked chopped bell pepper and corn kernels.) Add the smoked paprika, salt and pepper. Cook for about 5 minutes, until the potatoes are slightly softened.

Pour in the coconut milk and vegetable broth and simmer for 15 to 20 more minutes. Using an immersion or high-speed blender, blend about half of the soup until smooth, pour it back into the pot and give it a good stir.

Serve with fresh chopped parsley and the reserved bell pepper and corn, if you saved them.

Leftovers keep well in the fridge for up to 1 week.

ROSEMARY GARLIC HASSELBACK POTATOES

I am a total potato head. I grew up in Maine, where we had some form of potatoes at least two meals a day. I love 'em! This recipe is a really easy dinner idea that looks much fancier and more impressive than the amount of work required to make it. Just a few ingredients and you're on your way to a delicious date night dinner or meatless Monday meal!

SERVES 2 TO 4

2 large russet potatoes (about 1 lb [450 g] each)

¼ cup (60 ml) olive oil

Salt and pepper, to taste

4 to 6 cloves garlic, minced

3 or 4 sprigs fresh rosemary, stems discarded, finely chopped, plus more for garnish

Preheat the oven to 425°F (218°C).

Thinly slice the potatoes three-fourths of the way through for the entire length of the potato.

Lay the potatoes in a cast-iron pan or on a lined baking sheet and brush all over with the olive oil. Sprinkle with salt and pepper and bake for 30 minutes.

Remove the potatoes from the oven, brush them generously with more olive oil and bake for 30 to 35 more minutes.

Remove the potatoes one last time from the oven and carefully sprinkle the garlic and rosemary all over, making sure to push most of it into the crevices of each slice. Bake for 10 to 15 more minutes, then serve immediately!

chapter six

BAKE SALE—WORTHY BAKED GOODS

Baking is a lot less forgiving than cooking. It's much more of an exact science and if you screw up just one thing, you can end up with flat cookies or underdeveloped bread loaves. That's why I took the guesswork out of each one of these recipes. They're great, and they'll work every time—which is a MUST when you're whipping up six batches of something for a bake sale! Easy sweets like my Oatmeal Cream Pies (page 114), Perfect Peanut Butter Cookies (page 122) and Double Fudge Mint Brownies (page 126) are perfect for those new to baking or someone looking for a vegan spin on a traditional baked good. There's something here for everyone. Looking for something just a little fancier? Head over to the "When Cookies Won't Cut It" section (page 131)!

OATMEAL CREAM PIES

I made this recipe for my little sister, Jade. When we were growing up, oatmeal cream pies were her FAVORITE sweet treat. I knew my version had to be good enough to pass her taste test, but also way better for you than the version sold on grocery store shelves. I called her as soon as I took a bite—SUCCESS! Chewy, sweet, stuffed with sweet cream frosting—you're gonna love 'em. Jade does!

MAKES 9 LARGE OR 18 SMALL CREAM PIES

COOKIES

2 tbsp (12 g) ground flax

6 tbsp (90 ml) warm water

1 cup (220 g) vegetable shortening

¾ cup (165 g) packed brown sugar

½ cup (100 g) granulated sugar

1 tsp vanilla

1½ cups (200 g) all-purpose flour

1 tsp baking soda

1 tsp cinnamon

½ tsp salt

3 cups (240 g) old-fashioned rolled oats

CREAM FILLING

2½ cups (325 g) powdered sugar

½ cup (110 g) vegetable shortening

1 tbsp (15 ml) unsweetened almond milk

½ tsp vanilla extract

Preheat the oven to 350°F (175°C). Line a baking sheet with parchment paper.

To make the cookies, combine the ground flax and warm water in a small bowl to gelatinize. Set aside.

Beat together the shortening, brown sugar, granulated sugar and vanilla until fluffy. Beat in the flax mixture and set aside.

In a medium mixing bowl, sift together the flour, baking soda, cinnamon and salt. Pour this into the bowl of wet ingredients, and stir the two together until a soft dough forms. Fold in the rolled oats until completely combined.

Scoop eighteen 2-inch (5-cm) balls of dough for large pies or thirty-six 1-inch (2.5-cm) balls of dough for smaller pies onto the prepared baking sheet. Bake for 13 to 15 minutes, until the cookies are firm around the edges. Move the cookies to a wire rack to cool completely.

While the cookies cool, prepare the cream filling by beating together the powdered sugar, shortening, milk and vanilla until fluffy. Keep it in the fridge until the cookies are cool.

When the cookies have cooled completely, spread 1 to 2 tablespoons (15 to 30 g) of the cream filling over half of the cookies, then top with the remaining cookies to form sandwiches.

Tip

These travel well, but the frosting does best in the fridge if the weather is warm.

MAPLE-GLAZED BANANA WALNUT SCONES

I love a good scone, but a good scone can be hard to find. Often they are far too dry or crumbly, or don't have enough flavor. These scones beat the rap—they're moist, rich, fluffy and full of crunchy walnuts! The maple glaze adds a touch of sweetness and tastes great with the banana nut combo.

MAKES 8

SCONES

2 cups (330 g) whole wheat pastry flour

1 tbsp (11 g) baking powder

1 tsp cinnamon

½ tsp ground ginger

¼ tsp ground nutmeg

½ tsp salt

6 tbsp (80 g) cold vegan butter

¾ cup (190 g) mashed banana

¼ cup (60 ml) unsweetened almond milk

2 tbsp (30 ml) maple syrup

1 tsp vanilla extract

¾ cup (90 g) walnuts, chopped

MAPLE GLAZE

½ cup (65 g) powdered sugar

2 tbsp (60 ml) maple syrup

¼ tsp vanilla extract

1 to 2 tbsp (15 to 30 ml) unsweetened almond milk

Chopped walnuts, for garnish

Preheat the oven to 425°F (218°C). Line a baking sheet with parchment paper.

To make the scones, in a large mixing bowl, whisk together the whole wheat pastry flour, baking powder, cinnamon, ginger, nutmeg and salt. Using a pastry cutter or fork, cut in the cold vegan butter until small crumbs form. Pour in the mashed banana, almond milk, maple syrup and vanilla and stir together with a wooden spoon until a dough forms. Fold in the chopped walnuts.

Turn out the dough onto a lightly floured surface and form a 1-inch (2.5-cm) thick disk. Cut the disk into 8 equal scone wedges, like a pizza. Place the scones on the prepared baking sheet and bake for 15 to 17 minutes, until golden.

Place the scones on a wire rack to cool.

Prepare the maple glaze by whisking together the powdered sugar, maple syrup, vanilla and milk in a small bowl. Drizzle the glaze over completely cooled scones and sprinkle with chopped walnuts. Enjoy!

CHOCOLATE CHIP COOKIE BARS

These bars are FREAKY good. Packed with protein from the peanut butter, they're basically a workout food . . . that's how that works, right? They're sweet, chewy, ooey-gooey and *very* worthy of your next girls' night Netflix marathon.

MAKES 12

---

1 cup (192 g) sugar

1 cup (180 g) peanut butter

¾ cup (180 ml) unsweetened almond milk

1 tsp vanilla extract

1½ cups (188 g) all-purpose flour

2 tsp (7 g) baking powder

¼ tsp salt

½ cup (100 g) vegan chocolate chips or chunks

Preheat the oven to 350°F (175°C). Line or grease an 8 x 8-inch (20 x 20-cm) baking dish and set aside.

In a stand mixer or large mixing bowl, beat together the sugar, peanut butter, milk and vanilla. Pour in the flour, baking powder and salt and beat until a stiff batter forms. Fold in the chocolate chips, then add the batter to the prepared baking dish, using a wooden spoon to press the batter evenly into the pan.

Bake for 20 to 25 minutes, then move to a wire rack to cool. Once completely cooled, cut into 12 equal bars and serve!

Tip

For denser, fudgier bars be sure to refrigerate the bars for at least 2 hours before eating.

NO-BAKE CHOCOLATE COOKIES

One of the best parts about growing up with a mom who worked at our elementary school was keeping the same hours. We'd come home after school and bake delicious homemade goodies together. My mom had a few go-to sweet treats she'd always make, and her No-Bake Chocolate Cookies were my favorite. They were sweet, rich, whipped up quickly and were something I could easily help with as a kid. I love them just as much now, and you're going to love how easy they are to make vegan-friendly.

MAKES 16 TO 20

1½ cups (288 g) sugar

½ cup (120 ml) unsweetened almond milk

½ cup (105 g) vegan butter

¼ cup (28 g) unsweetened cocoa powder

½ cup (145 g) Creamy Cashew Vanilla Butter (page 182) or substitute peanut butter

1 tsp vanilla extract

3 cups (240 g) old-fashioned oats

In a large saucepan, whisk together the sugar, milk, butter and cocoa powder over medium heat. Bring the mixture to a boil for 60 to 90 seconds. Remove from the heat, and stir in the nut butter, vanilla and oats.

Scoop 1-inch (2.5-cm) balls of the mixture (they will spread out on their own) onto a parchment-lined baking sheet and let the cookies set and harden for at least 30 minutes. If the cookies have trouble hardening at all, you can move them to the fridge to firm up. Once they've set, eat 'em up!

Tip

You can use smooth or chunky peanut butter here—your choice!

PERFECT PEANUT BUTTER COOKIES

This is the perfect peanut butter cookie recipe. I might be biased, but seriously—chewy on the inside, a little crunchy on the outside, sugary, rich and packed with peanut butter—they check all the boxes! This is my favorite cookie recipe to date, and I can't wait for you to try them, too. They take traditional peanut butter cookies and blow them outta the water. And just wait 'til you see how we use them in the Peanut Butter Cookies + Cream Milkshake (page 158)!

MAKES 24

1 tbsp (6 g) ground flax

3 tbsp (45 ml) warm water

½ cup (105 g) cold vegan butter

1 cup (192 g) granulated sugar, divided

⅓ cup (48 g) packed brown sugar

3 tbsp (45 ml) unsweetened almond milk

1 tsp vanilla extract

¾ cup (135 g) smooth or chunky peanut butter

1¾ cups (219 g) all-purpose flour

1 tsp baking soda

½ tsp salt

⅛ tsp ground nutmeg

Combine the flax and warm water in a small bowl and set aside to thicken.

Add the butter, ½ cup (96 g) of the granulated sugar and brown sugar to a large bowl or stand mixer and beat until fluffy. Add the flax mixture, milk, vanilla and peanut butter. Beat the mixture for another 2 to 3 minutes or so, until it is well incorporated and fluffy.

In a separate mixing bowl, sift together the flour, baking soda, salt and ground nutmeg. Pour this mixture into the wet ingredients and mix until just combined. Cover the bowl and refrigerate the dough for at least 30 minutes.

While the dough chills, preheat the oven to 350°F (175°C) and line a baking sheet with parchment paper. Pour the remaining ½ cup (96 g) sugar into a small bowl.

Take the dough from the fridge and scoop out 1-inch (2.5-cm) balls. Roll them in the sugar and place them onto the baking sheet, using a fork to flatten them.

Bake for 10 to 12 minutes, until golden. Cool on a wire rack before serving.

Tip

If your dough seems crumbly at all at the end, simply add a few drops of milk at a time until it comes together.

CARROT CUPCAKES WITH ORANGE VANILLA CREAM FROSTING

I LOVE carrot cake and these cupcakes will have you loving it, too! These cupcakes bake up light, fluffy and moist, and are topped with the most delicious orange creamsicle-inspired frosting. Make them for someone you really love or hoard them all for yourself—I won't tell anyone!

MAKES 18

CUPCAKES

2 cups (260 g) whole wheat pastry flour

1 tbsp (11 g) baking powder

1 tsp baking soda

1 tsp salt

½ tsp cinnamon

½ tsp ground ginger

½ tsp nutmeg

1 cup (240 ml) unsweetened almond milk

1 cup (192 g) granulated sugar

½ cup (120 g) mashed banana

½ cup (120 ml) coconut oil, melted

2 tbsp (12 g) ground flax

2 tsp (10 ml) vanilla extract

2 cups (100 g) grated carrot

FROSTING

⅓ cup (90 g) cold vegan butter

2 tbsp (30 ml) orange juice

1 tsp orange zest

1 tsp vanilla extract

2 cups (260 g) powdered sugar

Chopped walnuts, for garnish (optional)

Preheat the oven to 350°F (175°C). Grease or line 18 cupcakes tins.

To make the cupcakes, in a medium bowl, sift together the flour, baking powder, baking soda, salt, cinnamon, ginger and nutmeg.

In a separate medium mixing bowl, whisk together the milk, granulated sugar, mashed banana, coconut oil, ground flax and vanilla. Add the dry ingredient mixture about a cup at a time, stirring to combine. Once the batter comes together, fold in the grated carrot.

Pour the batter into the greased or lined cupcake tins until the cups are three-fourths full. Bake for 25 to 30 minutes, or until an inserted toothpick comes out clean. Let cool completely on a wire rack.

While the cupcakes cool, prepare the frosting by beating together the cold butter, orange juice, orange zest and vanilla. Pour in the powdered sugar about a cup (130 g) at a time and beat until creamy. Move to the fridge to chill.

When the cupcakes have cooled, generously spread each one with a layer of the creamy orange vanilla frosting. Sprinkle with a garnish of chopped walnuts and enjoy!

Tip

Leftover cupcakes are best stored in the fridge or a cool place so the buttercream-like frosting doesn't melt.

DOUBLE FUDGE MINT BROWNIES

I am a total chocoholic, and I'm a real sucker for the combination of chocolate and mint. I knew I needed to put a recipe in here that had them both, because it's just such a great pairing. So I decided to try and make the world's fudgiest brownies. Success? I think so! I haven't tried all the brownies in the world, but I think these are a serious contender. They're rich, sweet, a little minty and seriously fudge-tastic—no eggs needed. Let's bake!

MAKES 12

½ cup (62 g) all-purpose flour

½ cup (50 g) whole wheat pastry flour

½ cup (56 g) cocoa powder

½ cup (96 g) sugar

2 tbsp (19 g) cornstarch

1 tsp baking powder

½ tsp salt

⅓ cup (90 ml) coconut oil, melted

½ cup (120 ml) maple syrup

¼ cup (60 ml) unsweetened almond milk

1 tsp vanilla extract

½ tsp peppermint extract

½ cup (100 g) vegan chocolate chips or chunks

Preheat the oven to 350°F (175°C). Grease or line an 8 x 8-inch (20 x 20-cm) baking dish.

In a large mixing bowl, whisk together the flours, cocoa powder, sugar, cornstarch, baking powder and salt.

In a separate mixing bowl, combine the melted coconut oil, maple syrup, unsweetened almond milk, and vanilla and peppermint extracts. Pour these wet ingredients into the dry ingredient mixture and use a wooden spoon to combine the mixture completely. The batter will be stiff, so feel free to get in there and use your hands if you like. Once the batter is uniform, pour in the chocolate chips and stir to evenly distribute them throughout the batter.

Press the mixture into the prepared baking dish, using the back of the wooden spoon to press it evenly into the dish. Bake for 20 to 25 minutes. If you bake them too long, they will become drier and much more cake-like than fudge-like in texture. Remove the dish from the oven and place it on a cooling rack to cool completely before slicing. For the ULTIMATE fudge brownies, see the tip below.

Once cooled, slice and enjoy!

Tips

Make these brownies EXTRA FUDGY by refrigerating them after cooling for at least 1 to 2 hours before slicing. The fridge helps cool the core before it has set completely, resulting in some of the best damn brownies ever!

If peppermint isn't your thing, you can leave the peppermint extract out altogether or replace it with an extract you like, such as almond or raspberry!

PUMPKIN WHOOPIE PIES

If you're not an East Coaster, you might be unfamiliar with what exactly a whoopie pie is. I've been making the traditional version—fluffy chocolate cakes filled with buttercream frosting—for years with my mom. There is even a chain of stores in Maine that ONLY sells dozens of varieties of them! While Maine, New Hampshire and Massachusetts all claim to be the original inventor, I like to believe they started in my home state. I know a great whoopie pie when I eat one, and these are GREAT whoopie pies. The pumpkin keeps the cakes moist and sweet and we stuffed 'em full of a rich, vegan buttercream that'll rival any you've had before.

MAKES 13 OR 14

WHOOPIE PIES

1 tbsp (6 g) ground flax

3 tbsp (45 ml) warm water

1 cup (220 g) packed brown sugar

½ cup (120 ml) coconut oil, melted

¾ cup (185 g) packed pumpkin puree

1 tsp vanilla extract

1½ cups (187 g) all-purpose flour

½ teaspoon baking soda

½ teaspoon baking powder

½ teaspoon salt

1 tbsp (6 g) pumpkin pie spice

¼ tsp cinnamon

¼ tsp ground ginger

¼ tsp nutmeg

BUTTERCREAM FILLING

1 cup (130 g) powdered sugar

½ cup (105 g) vegan butter

1 tbsp (15 ml) unsweetened almond milk

½ tsp vanilla extract

To make the whoopie pies, in a small bowl, whisk together the ground flax and warm water and set aside to gelatinize.

In a stand mixer or large bowl, beat together the brown sugar and coconut oil. Pour in the gelatinized flax mixture, pumpkin puree and vanilla and stir to combine.

In a separate mixing bowl, whisk together the flour, baking soda, baking powder, salt, pumpkin pie spice, cinnamon, ginger and nutmeg.

Pour the dry ingredient mixture into the wet ingredients, stirring continuously until a batter forms. Set the bowl aside while you preheat the oven to 350°F (175°C).

When the oven is ready, line a baking sheet with parchment paper. Drop tablespoons of batter onto the paper several inches apart—they will spread as they cook. You will need 26 to 28 cookies.

Bake for 10 to 12 minutes, or until the whoopie pies have become golden. Remove from the oven and move the cakes to a wire rack to cool.

While they cool, prepare the buttercream filling by creaming together the powdered sugar and butter. Add in the almond milk and vanilla and beat until fluffy. Spread or pipe the frosting evenly onto half of the cooled cakes, then top with the remaining half of the unfrosted cakes to make the whoopie pies. Enjoy!

Leftover whoopie pies are best saved in an airtight container or wrapped in plastic wrap and kept on the counter for up to 3 days.

chapter seven

WHEN COOKIES WON'T CUT IT

Like it says, sometimes cookies just won't cut it! Whether you're trying to impress your mother-in-law, your co-workers, your significant other or you're just fancy, you'll LOVE these next-level baked goods. With easier treats like Needhams (Potato) Candy (page 140) and Blueberry Crumb Cake (page 135) to fancier, trickier sweets like Strawberry Basil Hand Pies (page 132) and Whiskey-Baked Persimmon Bread Pudding (page 139), you'll be able to find something so good it's worth going back for seconds. All you need is an oven and some sweet, sweet resolve.

STRAWBERRY BASIL HAND PIES

These are maybe one of the yummiest things I've ever made. They take a little work, but they are so, SO worth it. Basically a healthier, adult-friendly pop tart, these sweet little guys are packed with fruit and drizzled with a sweet vanilla glaze. They're buttery and rich and taste WAY BETTER than store-bought.

MAKES 6

HAND PIES

1 heaping cup (210 g) sliced fresh or frozen strawberries

1 tbsp (15 ml) water (only if using fresh berries)

1 tbsp (3 g) finely chopped fresh basil

1 tsp sugar

1 tsp cornstarch

2 cups (260 g) whole wheat pastry flour

⅛ tsp salt

⅔ cup (150 g) cold vegan butter

2 to 4 tbsp (30 to 60 ml) ice water

VANILLA GLAZE

6 tbsp (49 g) powdered sugar

¼ tsp vanilla extract

1 to 3 tsp (5 to 15 ml) unsweetened almond milk

Tip

You can sub in any berries you prefer here, and if basil isn't for you, go ahead and leave it out.

Preheat the oven to 375°F (191°C). Line a baking sheet with parchment paper.

To make the hand pies, place the strawberries, water (only if using fresh berries), basil, sugar and cornstarch in a small saucepan over medium heat. Cook for 5 to 8 minutes, stirring occasionally and smashing down the fruit as it cooks. Remove from the heat and set aside.

In a large bowl, mix together the flour and salt. Cut in the cold butter with a fork or pastry cutter until small crumbs form. Drizzle the ice water over the mixture about 1 tablespoon (15 ml) at a time, mixing with a wooden spoon, until a dough begins to form. The dough should be moist but not sticky.

Turn out the dough onto a lightly floured surface and shape it into a disk. Use a rolling pin to roll the dough into a large, ¼-inch (6-mm) thick rectangle. Use a sheet of plastic wrap over the dough to prevent cracking as you roll it out, if needed. Cut the rectangle into 12 equal squares (or rectangles) and move half of them to the lined baking sheet.

Scoop about 1 tablespoon (15 g) of filling onto the 6 remaining squares, leaving about ¼ inch (6 mm) of space around the edges. Using your finger, dab a bit of water around the edges to help seal them. Top each square with its matching other half, pressing around the edges with a fork to seal them.

Use a toothpick to poke a poke a few small holes in the top, then bake for 20 to 25 minutes, or until golden brown.

While they cook, prepare the glaze by mixing together the powdered sugar, vanilla and unsweetened almond milk.

When the hand pies are finished, let them cool on a wire rack for 5 to 10 minutes before topping with the glaze.

BLUEBERRY CRUMB CAKE

My aunt is FAMOUS for her blueberry cake. In Maine we grow these super sweet, tiny, purple blueberries that she uses—I think they would make any cake taste good. I have a hard time getting my hands on them here on the West Coast, but if you can get them, use them! Especially in this cake. It's moist, sweet and sprinkled with a crunchy cinnamon crumb topping . . . I think my aunt will be impressed.

SERVES 12

BLUEBERRY CAKE

2 cups (260 g) whole wheat flour

1 tsp baking powder

1 tsp baking soda

½ tsp salt

⅓ cup (74 g) vegan butter

¾ cup (144 g) sugar

Zest of 1 lemon

½ cup (130 g) Homemade Applesauce (page 181), or store-bought

½ cup (120 ml) unsweetened almond milk

1 tsp vanilla extract

1½ cups (240 g) fresh blueberries

CRUMB TOPPING

½ cup (100 g) sugar

¼ cup (33 g) whole wheat flour

1 tsp cinnamon

⅛ tsp salt

¼ cup (60 g) vegan butter

Preheat the oven to 350°F (175°C).

To make the cake, in a large mixing bowl, combine the flour, baking powder, baking soda and salt. Set aside.

In a separate large mixing bowl, cream together the vegan butter, sugar and lemon zest. Mix in the applesauce, milk and vanilla until completely combined.

Pour the dry ingredients into the wet about a cup (120 g) at a time, stirring continuously until a stiff batter forms. Fold in the blueberries gently. Pour the batter into a greased or lined 8 x 8-inch (20 x 20-cm) baking dish and set aside while you make the crumb topping.

To make the crumb topping, whisk together the sugar, flour, cinnamon and salt. Using a fork, mash the vegan butter in until small crumbs form. Pour the crumb topping evenly over the blueberry cake batter. Bake for 40 to 45 minutes, until an inserted toothpick comes clean. Let cool completely before cutting and serving.

Leftover cake will stay fresh in the fridge for up to 3 days.

WHOLE WHEAT CINNAMON SUGAR PULL-APART LOAF

If you're looking for a brunch main that will totally impress your guests, you've come to the right place. This pull-apart loaf is super sharable and looks like you had to go to pastry school to learn to construct it. But I swear—it's really easy! Just make the dough, cover it in cinnamon sugar, slice and bake.

SERVES 4 TO 6

LOAF

2¼ tsp (7 g) active dry yeast

1¼ cups (300 ml) warm water

2 cups (250 g) all-purpose flour

1½ cups (195 g) whole wheat pastry flour

¼ cup (50 g) sugar

⅛ tsp salt

1 tbsp (15 ml) olive oil

FILLING

1 cup (200 g) sugar

2 tsp (6 g) cinnamon

½ tsp freshly ground nutmeg

4 tbsp (60 g) vegan butter

Preheat the oven to 350°F (175°C). Lightly grease a loaf pan and set aside.

To make the loaf, mix the active dry yeast into the warm water and set aside.

In a stand mixer fitted with a dough hook, mix together the all-purpose flour, whole wheat pastry flour, sugar, salt, olive oil and yeast mixture. Knead the mixture on medium speed until the dough is smooth and well incorporated. It shouldn't be too sticky, but you may add a few drops of water as needed if it seems too dry.

Form the dough into a ball and place in a large, lightly greased mixing bowl. Cover the bowl with plastic wrap or a clean dish towel and place it somewhere warm to double in size—1 to 2 hours.

While the dough rises, you can prepare the cinnamon sugar filling by whisking together the sugar, cinnamon and ground nutmeg in a small bowl. In a separate small bowl, melt the vegan butter. Set them aside.

Once the dough has risen, turn it out onto a lightly floured surface and use a rolling pin to roll the dough to about 12 x 20-inches (30 x 51-cm).

Brush the rolled-out dough evenly with the melted butter and spread the entirety of the cinnamon sugar mixture over the top.

Using a pizza cutter or pastry knife, cut the dough into 6 long strips lengthwise. Stack the strips and slice into 6 even stacks. Lay the stacks on their sides in the greased loaf pan.

Bake for 35 to 40 minutes, until golden. Pull from the oven and let cool before enjoying.

WHISKEY-BAKED PERSIMMON BREAD PUDDING

Bread pudding is just the worst name. It sounds like a soggy, sweetened, pureed loaf of bread and it deserves SO much more credit than that. This hearty bread pudding is stuffed with spiced, whiskey-baked persimmons and tossed in a rich coconut cream mixture before baking. It's a super impressive-looking and tasty treat, and is a great way to explore using sweet, seasonal persimmons. Persimmons not in season? Try using your favorite stone fruit instead!

SERVES 6

6 heaping cups (375 g) cubed stale French bread

4 persimmons, halved and thinly sliced

⅓ cup (80 ml) whiskey

1 tsp coconut oil

1 tbsp (12 g) sugar

1 tsp ground ginger, divided

½ tsp ground nutmeg, plus more for garnish

⅛ tsp cardamom

1 (14-oz [414-ml]) can full-fat coconut milk

1 cup (240 ml) unsweetened almond milk

¼ cup (60 ml) maple syrup

1 tsp vanilla extract

½ tsp ground cinnamon

¼ cup (38 g) cornstarch

Preheat the oven to 350°F (175°C). Grease a 9 x 13-inch (23 x 33-cm) baking dish.

Place the stale bread cubes in a large bowl and set aside.

In a medium-size baking dish, toss together the persimmons, whiskey, coconut oil, sugar, ½ teaspoon of the ginger, nutmeg and cardamom. Bake for 20 minutes, tossing again about halfway through.

While the persimmons are cooking, whisk together the coconut milk, almond milk, maple syrup, vanilla, cinnamon, remaining ½ teaspoon ginger and cornstarch in a saucepan. Cook over medium-low heat for 10 minutes, stirring frequently, until the mixture thickens.

Once finished, pour the coconut milk mixture and the whiskey baked persimmons over the bread in the large mixing bowl. Mix to combine everything evenly, then pour the mixture into the prepared baking dish. Let it sit for at least 20 minutes, then bake for 15 to 20 minutes. Serve immediately!

Leftovers keep well in the fridge for up to 1 week.

NEEDHAMS (POTATO) CANDY

Growing up in Maine meant eating potatoes with almost every meal. They're a huge crop for the state, and I still eat them several times a week. I LOVE potatoes! Any way you cook 'em, really. I can't remember the first time I had needhams (pronounced NEED-uhms), but I remember the first time I realized I could make them at home, from scratch, using only vegan ingredients. They're really easy to make and I swear you don't taste any potato—it's just there to add creaminess. You're gonna love 'em!

MAKES 20

2 cups (260 g) powdered sugar

¼ cup (75 g) plain mashed potatoes

1 tbsp (6 g) vegan butter

1 tsp vanilla extract

⅛ tsp salt

¾ cup (68 g) unsweetened, finely shredded coconut

½ lb (227 g) vegan chocolate chips or chopped bar chocolate

1 tbsp (11 g) coconut oil

Using a large saucepan with a glass bowl or another pan over the top, create a double boiler. Pour the powdered sugar into the glass bowl, creating a well in the middle. Add the mashed potatoes, butter, vanilla and salt to the well, gradually stirring the powdered sugar in until a smooth paste forms, about 5 minutes. Remove from the heat and stir in the shredded coconut. Pour the mixture into 20 small candy molds or form the mixture into a large, 1-inch (2.5-cm) thick square on a baking sheet. Place the candy molds or baking sheet in the freezer to harden, at least 20 minutes.

While the candies harden, use the same double boiler method to melt together the chocolate and coconut oil. When the candies have set, pop them out of the molds (or if using the baking sheet method, cut into 20 equal squares). Dip each square into the melted chocolate mixture, coating it completely. Place the coated candies onto a baking sheet in the fridge or freezer to set, about 1 hour. Enjoy!

Leftover candies will keep for up to 2 weeks in an airtight container in the fridge and indefinitely in the freezer.

LAVENDER SHORTCAKES

These lavender shortcakes are the perfect spring or summer dessert! Heaped with fresh fruit and coconut whip, they're a treat worthy of breakfast or dessert. They're light and fluffy and aren't too flowery or floral in taste. You'll be surprised how easy they are to whip up!

SERVES 6 TO 8

2 cups (250 g) all-purpose flour

1 tbsp (12 g) baking powder

1 tsp salt

¼ cup (60 g) coconut oil or vegan butter, at room temperature

¾ cup (180 ml) unsweetened almond milk

2 tbsp (24 g) sugar

2 tbsp (6 g) dried culinary lavender

Fresh seasonal fruit, for garnish

Coconut Whipped Cream (page 185), for garnish

Preheat the oven to 425°F (218°C). Line a baking sheet with parchment paper.

In a medium-size mixing bowl, combine the flour, baking powder and salt. Use a pastry cutter or fork to cut in the coconut oil until small crumbs form.

Stir in the milk, sugar and lavender using a wooden spoon until a soft dough forms. Knead the mixture several times, until just combined.

Turn out the dough onto a lightly floured surface and gently roll it out to about ½- to ¾-inch (13- to 19-mm) thick. Use a biscuit butter, thin-edged drinking glass or martini shaker to cut out the biscuits. You should get 6 to 8. Move the cut biscuits to the lined baking sheet.

Bake for 10 minutes, or until the biscuits have risen slightly and are becoming golden on top. Remove and let cool for least 5 minutes. Serve with fresh fruit and coconut whipped cream!

Tip

Use whatever fruit is in season! Strawberries and other berries pair really nicely with the lavender flavor.

ICE CREAM SANDWICH BARS

I love the combination of soft chocolate cookie and sweet vanilla ice cream that makes a traditional ice cream sandwich. The cookies have to be soft and melt in your mouth or you're stuck chewing through a tough cookie or having to bite so hard the ice cream smooshes out the back of the sandwich. These are the PERFECT replacement for those old-school bars. The chocolate cookies are moist and really do melt in your mouth—they're more like cookie biscuits—and paired with my Creamy Vanilla Bean Ice Cream (page 147), they'll take you right back to childhood.

MAKES 6 LARGE OR 12 SMALL

About 4 cups (1.4 kg) Creamy Vanilla Bean Ice Cream (page 147)

½ cup (115 g) vegan butter

½ cup (96 g) sugar

⅓ cup (90 g) Homemade Applesauce (page 181), or store-bought

1 tsp vanilla extract

½ cup (63 g) all-purpose flour

¼ cup (28 g) cocoa powder

½ tsp salt

Preheat the oven to 350°F (175°C). Line a half baking sheet or jelly-roll pan with parchment paper. Move your ice cream to the refrigerator or countertop to soften while you work on the cookies.

In a medium-size bowl or stand mixer, cream together the butter and sugar. Pour in the applesauce and vanilla and stir to combine.

In a separate medium-size bowl, whisk together the flour, cocoa powder and salt. Pour the dry ingredients into the wet, stirring until completely combined. Spread the batter onto the prepared baking sheet or jelly-roll pan.

Bake for 10 to 12 minutes, until the cake is dry to the touch and pulling away from the edges of the pan. When completely cooled, lift the parchment paper gently and move the cake to a flat work surface. Cut the cake in half width-wise using a serrated knife.

Place one half of the cake, flat side down, on a large piece of plastic wrap. Spread the ice cream evenly over the layer, then top with the second half of the cake, flat side up. Fold the plastic wrap around the rest of the ice cream sandwich tightly but gently. Place the sandwich back on the pan and place it in the freezer until firm, at least 3 hours.

When ready, unwrap the plastic wrap and place the ice cream sandwich on a large cutting board. Using a serrated knife, cut into 6 large or 12 small ice cream sandwiches, wiping off the blade between each cut. Serve immediately or save in the freezer!

Tip

If you don't feel like making ice cream, you can always substitute the ice cream layer with your favorite store-bought brand. You'll need about 2 pints (1 kg).

CREAMY VANILLA BEAN ICE CREAM

The secret to creamy, fluffy, coconut-based ice cream without an ice cream maker? Date paste and lots of stirring! Incorporating air into the mixture keeps the ice cream light, and the date paste is like a magical ingredient that won't completely freeze, keeping the mixture much more scoopable and more enjoyable to eat. It's great on its own and perfect stuffed into Ice Cream Sandwich Bars (page 144) or Peanut Butter Cookies + Cream Milkshakes (page 158). Yum!

MAKES ABOUT 4 CUPS (2 PINTS)

1 cup (170 g) pitted Medjool dates

1 to 4 tbsp (15 to 60 ml) hot water

2 (14-oz [414-ml]) cans full-fat coconut cream or 4 (14-oz [414-ml]) cans full-fat coconut milk, liquid drained

½ cup (120 ml) unsweetened almond milk

3 vanilla beans, scraped

Place a large mixing bowl in the freezer to chill.

In a small bowl, soak the pitted dates in hot water to cover for about 10 minutes, until the dates have softened. Drain and place the soaked dates into a food processor. Pour in the hot water, 1 tablespoon (15 ml) at a time, and process until a smooth paste forms. Scoop the paste into a small bowl and set aside.

Place the coconut cream into the chilled mixing bowl and whip with beaters until it becomes light and airy. Add in the unsweetened almond milk, vanilla bean scrapings and date paste. Beat together until the mixture is fluffy and fully incorporated.

Cover the bowl with plastic wrap and place in the freezer for at least 4 hours. Pull it out and give it a good stir about every hour or so, to incorporate air.

Scoop into a bowl and serve! Keeps in the freezer indefinitely.

chapter eight

HAVE A DRINK

From Rosemary Coconut Hot Chocolate (page 161) to Strawberry Rhubarb Shrub (page 153) and—my favorite—Peanut Butter Cookies + Cream Milkshake (page 158), I've got something you can serve up at any occasion. More of a lemonade lady? I got you, girl. Get out your fancy glasses and some stir sticks—I'm on a mission to quench your thirst and re-create old favorites!

SPARKLING MINT LEMONADE

This lemonade packs a ton of fresh flavor and the addition of ginger beer gives it an extra kick! It's perfect for poolside sipping and is a great nonalcoholic fancy drink to serve at parties or with friends. Add a little alcohol, if you like!

SERVES 2

1 cup (240 ml) freshly squeezed lemon juice

½ cup (120 ml) nonalcoholic ginger beer

½ cup (12 g) packed fresh mint leaves, plus more for garnish

4 tbsp (50 g) sugar

2 cups (480 ml) sparkling mineral water

2 to 3 cups (320 to 480 g) ice

Lemon slices, for garnish

Combine all of the ingredients—except for the garnishes—in a high-speed blender until smooth, cracking the top just slightly while blending to release the air pressure inside. Serve with lemon slices and fresh mint sprigs!

Tip

If your blender doesn't allow for air to be released while blending, blend everything BUT the sparkling water together and just stir that in afterward to avoid a blender-spolsion!

STRAWBERRY RHUBARB SHRUB

I love kombucha, but I hate waiting for it to ferment. It takes at least 10 days and sometimes I just don't want to wait! This spin on an old-fashioned shrub is the perfect solution. It's ready in 24 hours, can be flavored to taste like almost anything and tastes great in sparkling water or mixed drinks. It's the mixer you didn't know you needed in your life!

MAKES 2 TO 3 CUPS (475 TO 700 ML)

1 cup (205 g) sliced strawberries

½ cup (100 g) thinly sliced rhubarb

1 cup (200 g) sugar

1 cup (240 ml) apple cider vinegar

Sparkling water, for serving

Mint leaves, for garnish

Place the strawberries and rhubarb in a medium-size bowl. Use a potato masher or wooden spoon to mash the berries so they release their juices. Pour the fruit into a large glass jar (3 cups [700 ml] or larger), followed by the sugar and apple cider vinegar. Put the lid on and shake the mixture vigorously, until the sugar has mostly dissolved.

Refrigerate the mixture overnight, shaking every few hours, until the sugar has completely dissolved.

The next day, strain the mixture through a cheesecloth over a pitcher until just fruit pulp remains. Toss the pulp, and pour the shrub mixture back into the jar. Place it back into the refrigerator for at least 1 day, to allow the flavors to combine and the mixture to slightly ferment. You can refrigerate it longer (up to 2 weeks), until your desired flavor develops.

Serve with sparkling water and fresh mint over ice, or use as a simple syrup to sweeten cocktails and mixed drinks.

When mixing with sparkling water to make a soda-like drink, I found that a ratio of about 3 tablespoons (45 ml) shrub syrup to 8 ounces (240 ml) sparkling water was perfect.

It will keep in an airtight container in the fridge indefinitely, though the flavor will continue to develop.

Tip

Substitute any fruit you like here! This shrub syrup is super versatile.

CHAMOMILE STEAMER

Buying tea lattes costs too much these days. It's rarely under $5, especially with the up-charge for nondairy milk. Who can afford that nonsense? Well, now you don't need to! This chamomile steamer is like the chai latte's cousin, but totally caffeine-free! Soothing and sweet, this drink is the perfect morning treat or nighttime sipper and is super easy to make yourself.

SERVES 1 OR 2

2 cups (480 ml) unsweetened almond milk

2 chamomile tea bags or 2 tbsp (10 g) loose-leaf tea in a strainer

2 tbsp (30 ml) maple syrup

⅛ tsp ground ginger

⅛ tsp freshly ground nutmeg

Chamomile flowers, for garnish (optional)

Heat the milk and tea in a medium-size saucepan until hot, but do not bring to a boil. Remove the tea bags or strainer and whisk in the maple syrup, ginger and nutmeg. Using a milk frother or high-speed blender, add your desired amount of foam to the drink. Serve immediately, garnished with chamomile flowers, if desired.

Tip
You can use any tea you like in place of the chamomile. Strong green, fruity black and earthy herbal teas all taste great!

HORCHATA

I didn't have horchata until I moved to California when I was 18. It was the best thing I had ever tasted. For someone who is lactose intolerant, it was a dream finding a sweet, milky drink that I could enjoy *without* getting a terrible stomachache. Traditionally, horchata is made from rice milk. You can go to the tiniest hole-in-the-wall Mexican restaurant here in LA and almost always find vegan, dairy-free horchata, still being made the traditional way. Rice milk alone tends to be watery, so I added almond milk to this recipe for a bit of creaminess, but you can leave it out if you want to keep the drink more traditional. Best served alongside a hearty plate of street tacos!

SERVES 4 TO 6

¾ cup (164 g) white rice

¾ cup (120 g) pitted Medjool dates

2 tsp (10 ml) vanilla extract

½ tsp ground cinnamon

4 cups (960 ml) water

1 cup (240 ml) unsweetened almond milk

Soak the white rice in hot water to cover for about 2 hours, until the rice is slightly softened. Drain the rice and pour it into a high speed blender.

Add the dates, vanilla, cinnamon and water and blend on high speed for 1 to 2 minutes, until the ingredients are completely emulsified. Pour the mixture into a bowl or pitcher covered in a cheesecloth and strain until only pulp remains in the cloth.

Stir the almond milk into the mixture, and place in the refrigerator to chill. Serve over ice.

Leftover horchata can be kept in the fridge for up to 1 week.

Tip

If you don't have dates on hand, feel free to substitute maple syrup, agave or your sweetener of choice.

PEANUT BUTTER COOKIES + CREAM MILKSHAKE

This milkshake brings all the boys to the yard. I used to consider any softened ice cream essentially a milkshake, but my partner, Alex, an aficionado, taught me otherwise. A great milkshake is a thick, creamy treat that is blended just to the point of perfection, then topped with crumbled cookies. The perfect milkshake requires the right ratio of ice cream to milk and with this recipe, I nailed it. My preference is 3:1 for ultimate creaminess—and creaminess is key!

SERVES 2

2 cups (425 g) Creamy Vanilla Bean Ice Cream (page 147)

⅔ cup (180 ml) unsweetened almond milk

4 Perfect Peanut Butter Cookies (page 122), crumbled

If you have access to a milkshake wand, throw your ingredients into a tall metal cup and froth away.

Otherwise, let your ice cream sit out for 5 to 10 minutes, to soften slightly. Scoop it into a high-speed blender. Add in the milk and 3 of the peanut butter cookies and start the blender on a very low speed until the ingredients combine and the cookies are crushed, 15 to 30 seconds. Pour into 2 tall, chilled glasses straight from the freezer, top with the last crumbled cookie and share with someone you like. Or don't, and eat it all up yourself. I won't say a word!

Tips

Freeze your glass first. This allows the temperature of the glass to cool down and keep your drink colder, longer. It also gives you that delicious-looking frosty glass to pour your milkshake into. Bloggers: It makes your photos look better.

Never add ice to your milkshake. Milkshakes are all about creaminess; adding ice is for smoothies.

ROSEMARY COCONUT HOT CHOCOLATE

There's nothing better on a cold winter's day than a big, warm mug of hot chocolate. Whether you're curled up watching a movie or are just enjoying watching the snow fall, it's the perfect way to enjoy the cooler weather. This hot chocolate is the ultimate creamy indulgence, subtly fragranced by the rosemary and made with rich coconut milk. If you want to cut fat, you can use any nondairy milk as a substitute, but the thickness of canned coconut milk really lends to the depth of this drink. Grab the (vegan) marshmallows!

SERVES 1 OR 2

1 (14-oz [414-ml]) can full-fat coconut milk

¼ cup (50 g) sugar

2 tbsp (14 g) cocoa powder

1 oz (28 g) vegan dark chocolate, chopped

1 tsp vanilla extract

Pinch of salt

2 or 3 sprigs fresh rosemary

Vegan marshmallows, for garnish (optional)

In a large saucepan over medium heat, whisk together the coconut milk, sugar, cocoa powder, chocolate, vanilla and salt. Once combined and the sugar has dissolved, place the rosemary sprigs in the mixture and simmer for 10 minutes, stirring occasionally. Remove the mixture from the heat, toss the used rosemary sprigs, and pour the hot chocolate into a large mug. Garnish with a fresh sprig of rosemary and vegan marshmallows, if you have 'em!

Tip

Rosemary not your favorite flavor? Leave it out completely for a traditional, creamy mug of hot cocoa or get creative and substitute it with a pinch of cinnamon or a teaspoon of peppermint extract.

HOLIDAY NOG

The best part of the holidays? All the sweet treats! The worst part of the holidays? All those damn sweet treats! Save the sugar for the cookies and make this naturally sweetened, rich, creamy Holiday Nog to satisfy your sweet tooth instead. It's free of eggs and much lighter than the original—guilt-free, too!

SERVES 2

½ cup (75 g) raw cashews

1 cup (240 ml) hot water

1½ cups (360 ml) unsweetened almond milk

1 cup (276 ml) canned, full-fat coconut milk

4 to 6 Medjool dates, pitted

1 tsp vanilla extract

¼ tsp ground cinnamon

⅛ tsp ground cloves

⅛ tsp salt

Rum (optional)

Whole cloves, for garnish

In a small bowl, soak the raw cashews in the hot water for at least 30 minutes. Drain.

Pour the soaked cashews, almond and coconut milks, dates, vanilla, cinnamon, cloves and salt into a high-speed blender and blend until creamy. You can strain it through cheesecloth if you like, but I love how creamy this drink is and didn't bother straining. Serve cold with rum (if you like!) and garnish with whole cloves.

Tip

This can easily be made the night before and left in the fridge until you're ready to serve it!

chapter nine

STOCK YOUR PANTRY

You could run to the store every time you need the vegan versions of your favorite milk, cheese and bread . . . or you could save yourself time and money by learning to make your own! In this section I break down the basics so you can spend more time at home cooking from scratch, and less time wondering if carrageenan will give you cancer someday. I even cover a few treats I bet you didn't know you could make on your own, like Eggless Mayo (page 178), Perfect Pizza Dough (page 169) and Creamy Cashew Vanilla Butter (page 182). Let's stock your pantry!

FLUFFY WHOLE WHEAT BISCUITS

I'm quickly becoming (am already?) the age where family meals are being held at my place and I'm expected to *wow* everyone at the dinner table. Sometimes it's the simplest dishes that make a meal great, and these fluffy, whole wheat biscuits are definitely a crowd-pleaser. They're the perfect amount of airy and buttery, and the whole wheat flour makes them a bit healthier and heartier than their white bread cousins. Best served warm and fresh from the oven, but equally as delicious smothered in gravy the next day!

MAKES 8

1 cup (240 ml) unsweetened almond milk

1 tbsp (15 ml) apple cider vinegar

1 cup (155 g) whole wheat flour

1 cup (155 g) whole wheat pastry flour

1 tbsp (10 g) baking powder

½ tsp baking soda

½ tsp sea salt

4 tbsp (60 g) cold vegan butter

2 tbsp (30 ml) melted vegan butter, for brushing

Preheat the oven to 450°F (232°C). Line a baking sheet with parchment.

In a glass measuring cup, combine the almond milk and vinegar. Set aside.

In a large mixing bowl, combine the flours, baking powder, baking soda and sea salt. Add the cold butter—best straight from the fridge—and use a fork or pastry cutter to cut it in until small crumbs form.

Make a well in the center and pour in half of the milk mixture. Mix gently with a wooden spoon, adding milk as needed until a dough forms—you may not need all of it. Stir until just combined. The mixture should be sticky.

Turn out the dough onto a lightly floured surface and gently turn the dough in on itself 4 or 5 times. Form the dough into a 1-inch (2.5-cm) thick disk, handling it as little as possible in the process.

Using a dough cutter or sharp round object—such as a drinking glass or cookie cutter—push straight down into the dough to cut out the biscuits. Gently twist to remove and repeat, gently reforming the dough as you go, until you've used all of the dough. You will have about 8 biscuits.

Place the biscuits in two rows on the baking sheet, making sure they are just touching—this helps them rise better in the oven. Brush the tops generously with the melted vegan butter and bake for 12 to 16 minutes, or until the biscuits are fluffy and slightly golden.

Enjoy warm with butter or cool with jam, or you know, one of a million other ways I'm sure you can think of to do with these delicious things!

Leftover biscuits can be stored in an airtight container.

Tip
Make sure your butter is very cold—straight from the fridge is best.

PERFECT PIZZA DOUGH

Alex is the King of All Things Pizza in this house, and he has officially declared this the "perfect pizza dough." And who am I to argue? It comes together pretty easily, creates a great crispy, chewy crust and makes enough dough for two pizzas—so you don't have to share. That makes it pretty perfect to me!

MAKES 2 DOUGHS

2¼ tsp (7 g) active dry yeast

1½ cups (360 ml) warm water

3½ cups (437 g) all-purpose flour, plus more as needed

2 tsp (6 g) salt

1 tsp sugar

2 tbsp (30 ml) olive oil

Pour the yeast and warm water into a small bowl and stir. Set aside for 5 minutes.

In a stand mixer, combine the flour, salt and sugar. Pour in the yeast mixture and the olive oil and, using the dough hook attachment, knead the mixture until it comes together and forms a ball. If the dough seems too sticky, add flour as needed. If it's too dry, add a bit of water.

Turn out the dough onto a lightly floured surface and knead into a smooth, firm ball. Grease the inside of the mixing bowl lightly and place the dough back inside. Cover with plastic wrap or a clean dish towel and leave in a warm place to double in size, 1 to 2 hours.

When ready, turn out the dough onto a lightly floured surface and, handling as little as possible, cut the dough into 2 equal pieces. Let them rest for 10 minutes before tossing and stretching for pizza!

Dough can be refrigerated for up to 2 days or frozen indefinitely.

HEMP SEED BASIL PESTO

Having a jar of pesto in the fridge is pretty much the same as having a pile of expensive jewelry in the closet—it's mealtime *gold*. Throw it on a pizza, or use it in pasta or as a sandwich spread and you're halfway to solving the weeknight dinner conundrum! Plus, it whips up in a flash and lasts a few weeks in the fridge, so you can make several meals out of just one batch.

MAKES ABOUT 2 CUPS (475 ML)

3 packed cups (165 g) fresh basil

½ cup (62 g) hemp seeds

3 tbsp (45 ml) lemon juice

3 cloves garlic

½ tsp salt

½ tbsp black pepper

½ cup (120 ml) olive or grapeseed oil

Rinse the basil and separate the leaves from the stems. Toss the stems in the compost and the leaves in a food processor or high-speed blender.

Add the hemp seeds, lemon juice, garlic, salt and pepper. Blend until smooth. Add the olive oil and blend again until evenly incorporated.

Store in a sealed container in the fridge for up to 2 weeks.

GARLIC HERB PIZZA + PASTA SAUCE

Making your own pizza and pasta sauce is easy and way cheaper than store-bought. Plus, it tastes WAY better! This sauce is packed with garlic and fresh herbs and is the perfect complement to any Italian dishes you whip up.

MAKES ABOUT 4 CUPS (950 ML)

2 tbsp (30 ml) olive oil

1 large onion, chopped

6 cloves garlic, minced

3 lb (1.4 kg) tomatoes, quartered

¼ cup (18 g) chopped fresh basil

2 tbsp (9 g) chopped fresh oregano

1 tsp salt

½ tsp pepper

¼ tsp crushed red pepper (optional)

Heat the olive oil in a large pot or Dutch oven over medium heat. Sauté the onion and garlic together until softened and fragrant, about 5 minutes.

Meanwhile, place the tomatoes in a food processor (you may need to do two batches depending on the size of your processor) and pulse until the tomatoes reach your desired texture. You can leave them a little chunky or blend until smooth.

Pour the tomato puree into the pot with the onions and garlic and add the basil, oregano, salt, pepper and crushed red pepper (if using). Simmer for 30 to 60 minutes, stirring occasionally, until the sauce thickens. The longer it cooks, the thicker it will become.

Serve on pizza, pasta and more! Leftover sauce can be canned or stored in an airtight container in the fridge for up to 2 weeks.

EASY CASHEW CHEESE

There used to be very few vegan cheeses on the market, and the ones that did exist were pretty crummy. There are some really great options these days, but they tend to be expensive and aren't always easy to find at regular grocery stores. When you want a cheaper, easier option or need to whip up some cheese quickly, try this recipe! It tastes great and is a delicious, homemade alternative to pricey store-bought faux cheese.

MAKES ABOUT 1 CUP (240 G)

1 cup (150 g) raw cashews

1 tbsp (15 ml) lemon juice

1 clove garlic

¼ tsp salt

¼ tsp pepper

2 to 4 tbsp (30 to 60 ml) water

Pour the raw cashews into a small bowl and add enough hot water to just cover the nuts. Soak for 30 minutes or more.

Drain the water and place the soaked cashews into a food processor or high-speed blender. Add the lemon juice, garlic clove, salt and pepper and begin to process them together. Add the water, 1 tablespoon (15 ml) at a time, until the desired consistency is reached. Serve with fresh chives and crusty bread for an easy appetizer!

Tip

Adjust the ingredients as needed to create a flavor you prefer. Try adding other flavors like smoked paprika, truffle salt, hot peppers or fresh herbs to mix it up!

HOMEMADE NUT MILK

Homemade nut milk is cheaper and easier to make than you might imagine. All you really need to do is blend nuts and water together—you can even add whatever flavors you like! This is a pantry staple that is better for you than the store-bought chemical versions and tastes way better, too!

MAKES ABOUT 4 CUPS (960 ML)

1 cup (150 g) raw almonds, cashews, macadamia nuts—it's your choice!

4 cups (960 ml) water

Pinch of salt

OTHER ADD-IN IDEAS

1 tsp vanilla or another flavored extract

1 tsp cinnamon, nutmeg, ginger or all of the above

1 to 2 tbsp (15 to 30 ml) maple syrup or agave nectar

A few pitted dates

Place the nuts, water, salt and any other add-ins in a high-speed blender and blend until the nuts have nearly dissolved, up to a couple of minutes.

Using cheesecloth or a nut milk bag, strain the milk into a large jug or pitcher, squeezing out the liquid as much as possible. Pour the remaining matter from the cheesecloth into the compost or trash.

Refrigerate the milk until cold, then enjoy! The milk will keep in the fridge for up to 1 week.

Tip
You can use whatever nuts you want to make milk with. Get creative!

EGGLESS MAYO

This recipe is the perfect substitute for pricey, store-bought vegan mayo. Sure, it takes a little time, but you'll be amazed by how creamy this mayo gets! It's made with ground flax instead of eggs, so it's completely cholesterol-free and preservative-free, too!

MAKES ABOUT 1 CUP (240 G)

3 tbsp (45 ml) water

1 tbsp (3 g) ground flax

1½ tsp (7 g) Dijon mustard

2 tbsp (30 ml) red wine vinegar or apple cider vinegar

½ tsp salt

¼ tsp garlic powder

¾ cup (180 ml) sunflower oil

Combine the water and flax in a small saucepan. Heat over medium heat, stirring constantly, until the mixture thickens and becomes gelatinous, 3 to 5 minutes.

Pour the mixture into a food processor. Add the Dijon, vinegar, salt and garlic powder. Begin processing on high speed, adding in 1 tablespoon (15 ml) sunflower oil and blending for 30 seconds. Pour in another tablespoon (15 ml) oil and continue blending for another 30 seconds. Repeat this process until all of the oil has been added and the mixture is creamy and whipped, like traditional mayo.

Because of the Dijon mustard and flax, the mayo will not be super white, but more of a yellowish color. It's still delicious!

Leftover mayo can be saved in an airtight container in the fridge for up to 1 week.

Tip

DO NOT add more than 1 tablespoon (15 ml) oil at a time. I'm repeating this here because it is ESSENTIAL to the success of this recipe.

HOMEMADE APPLESAUCE

Homemade applesauce is such an easy thing to make! It's a "set it and forget it" kind of recipe, and it's the perfect way to preserve apples long after they've lost their crispness. You can easily adjust the flavors to suit your tastes, and if you're into canning, this is the perfect recipe to get you started. Applesauce is the perfect baking binder replacement for eggs in vegan recipes, so it's always good to have some on hand. Plus, it'll leave your house smelling AMAZING!

MAKES ABOUT 6 CUPS (1.4 KG)

5 lb (2.3 kg) apples, cored and cut into 1" (2.5 cm) chunks (peeling is optional!)

1 cup (240 ml) water

3 tbsp (45 ml) lemon juice

2 cinnamon sticks or 2 tsp (5 g) ground cinnamon

2 tbsp (28 g) packed brown sugar

Place all of the ingredients in a large pot and cook over medium heat, stirring occasionally, for 45 to 60 minutes, until the apples have completely softened and mostly broken down. Use a potato masher (for chunkier applesauce), an immersion blender (for some chunks) or a food processor (for smooth applesauce) to reach the desired consistency, then enjoy!

Leftovers will keep in the fridge for about 2 weeks in an airtight container.

CREAMY CASHEW VANILLA BUTTER

This nut butter tastes like dessert. Spread it on toast, fruit or ice cream or just eat it by the spoonful. It's packed with healthy fats and protein and is SO good, you'll want to smear it on everything!

MAKES ABOUT 1 CUP (240 G)

---

2 cups (300 g) raw cashews

1 vanilla bean, scraped

¼ tsp cinnamon

Pinch of salt

Preheat the oven to 325°F (163°C). Line a baking sheet with parchment paper.

Spread the cashews on the baking sheet and roast for 10 to 15 minutes, stirring once, until golden and fragrant.

Let the cashews cool completely, then pour them into a food processor with the vanilla bean scrapings, cinnamon and salt and process until smooth. It might take a while—it took me about 5 continuous minutes of processing to get a super smooth consistency. Of course, if you prefer it a little chunky, you do you—just stop processing while there are still some chunks left.

Your nut butter doesn't need to be refrigerated, and should keep for at least 2 weeks out of the fridge. It will last indefinitely in the fridge.

COCONUT WHIPPED CREAM

This easy-to-make topping has become a staple in our refrigerator. I put it on hot drinks and sweet treats and sometimes enjoy it just by the spoonful. It's so easy to make and way cheaper than store-bought, soy-based versions.

MAKES ABOUT 1 CUP (240 G)

1 (14-oz [414-ml]) can full-fat coconut milk

3 to 6 tbsp (30 to 60 g) powdered sugar

1 to 2 tsp (5 to 10 ml) vanilla extract

Refrigerate the canned coconut milk overnight, being careful not to shake or jostle the can.

Once you're ready to make the whip, gently open the can and use a spoon to remove the thick white layer of coconut cream from the top half of the can. Discard the leftover clearish liquid left at the bottom or save for another use.

Put the thick white cream into a mixing bowl with the sugar and vanilla. Mix with hand beaters until the mixture is smooth, creamy and fluffy!

Leftovers can be refrigerated for several days, re-fluffing with beaters if necessary.

ACKNOWLDEDGMENTS

First I'd like to thank my mom and dad for always encouraging my sister, Jade, and me to help in the kitchen and for getting us excited about growing our own food. You've instilled in me such a reverence and respect for where my food comes from and how it brings people together, and I am forever grateful for your encouraging me to follow my dreams. I love you both!

I'm again super grateful to my life partner, Alex, and his willingness to try every dish I whip up. He's an honest taste tester and has been incredibly supportive of every crazy idea I've come up with. I'll love you to the mountains and back.

Huge hugs to my friends (Nat, Amy, Terry and Felicia) for whisking me away on a girls' trip the weekend before this was due to save my sanity and give me such encouraging, positive feedback. I'm so lucky to have friends like you.

To all the people who read and follow my recipes online and now in print—you are everything. It means the world to me to have you along for the ride.

And of course, to my pals Marissa and Meg B at Page Street, who turned this labor of love into a real, respectable cookbook.

ABOUT THE AUTHOR

Amber St. Peter is a full-time blogger and cookbook author living in sunny Southern California with her partner, Alex, and pitbull pup, Maddie. She spends her days cooking in her tiny bungalow kitchen, running or doing yoga with the dog, and nerding out on comic books. She also blogs regularly at FettleVegan.com, where she brags that she makes a damn good chocolate chip cookie. And she does.

INDEX